Lernkrimi Englisch

Death at Land's End

Lillian Flint
Caroline Simpson

W0236836

compact

Weitere Informationen zu Compact Lernkrimis finden Sie am Ende des Buches und unter www.lernkrimi.de.

© Compact Verlag GmbH
Baierbrunner Straße 27, 81379 München
Ausgabe 2015

Alle Rechte vorbehalten. Nachdruck, auch auszugsweise,
nur mit ausdrücklicher Genehmigung des Verlages gestattet.

Chefredaktion: Dr. Matthias Feldbaum
Redaktion: Helga Aichele
Fachkorrektur: Nathalie Russell
Produktion: Ute Hausleiter
Titelillustration: Karl Knospe
Lernkrimi-Logo: Carsten Abelbeck
Gestaltung: EKH Werbeagentur GbR, textum GmbH
Umschlaggestaltung: EKH Werbeagentur GbR, Hartmut Baier

ISBN 978-3-8174-9658-7
381749658/1

www.compactverlag.de, www.lernkrimi.de

# Vorwort

Liebe Leserin, lieber Leser,

sicher zum Lernerfolg – mit Spaß und Spannung! Die Compact Lernkrimis mit ihrer Kombination aus Lektüre und didaktischem Übungsanteil eignen sich hervorragend, um breite Sprachkompetenzen in der Fremdsprache zu erwerben. Der Lerner wird dabei durch die spannende Handlung, das angemessene Sprachniveau und den stetig ansteigenden Schwierigkeitsgrad der Übungen gefördert und motiviert.

Entwickelt nach neuesten Erkenntnissen der Fremdsprachendidaktik, sind Compact Lernkrimis das ideale Medium für einen Lernerfolg im Selbststudium. Durch die kleinen Texteinheiten und den hohen Übungsanteil sind sie aber auch als Unterrichtslektüre bestens geeignet.

So lernen Sie mit Compact Lernkrimis:
- **Mit Begeisterung lernen:** Die packende Krimihandlung motiviert Sie beim Lesen des englischen Originaltextes.
- **Wissen intensivieren und erweitern:** Durch die Kombination aus didaktisierter Lektüre und textbezogenen Übungen testen und trainieren Sie Ihre Sprachkenntnisse effektiv. Vokabelangaben auf jeder Seite unterstützen Sie beim Lesen.
- **Systematisch lernen:** Knüpfen Sie an Ihr individuelles Sprachniveau an und setzen Sie eigene Lernziele – linear im Schwierigkeitsgrad ansteigend oder mit punktuellen Schwerpunkten von Grundwortschatz bis Hörverstehen.
- **Unabhängig sein:** Lernen Sie ganz individuell – wo und wann Sie wollen.

Viel Spaß beim **spannend Englisch lernen**
wünscht Ihnen

Prof. Dr. Christiane Neveling
Didaktik der romanischen Sprachen, Universität Leipzig

Inhalt

Die Ereignisse und die handelnden Personen in diesem Buch sind frei erfunden. Etwaige Ähnlichkeiten mit tatsächlichen Ereignissen oder lebenden Personen wären rein zufällig und unbeabsichtigt.

Death at Land's End

Caroline Simpson

The Jolly Roger

It's a lovely summer day. Anne Sophie is sitting on the **harbour** wall in Sennen Cove, Cornwall.ⓘ She is writing a postcard to her family in Heidelberg.

Wednesday, 9th July, 2014. Dear Mum and Dad, I am writing to you in English for practice :-) My au pair job is still going well. Mr and Mrs Barber are very friendly. The children are noisy but sweet! This week we are on holiday in Cornwall. It's very beautiful here at the seaside...

harbour	Hafen
for practice	zum Üben
noisy	laut
at the seaside	an der Küste
except (for)	bis auf, außer
sailor	Matrose
pipe	Tabakspfeife

It's so peaceful, she thinks. There is no one else at the harbour, **except for** an old man who is cleaning one of the yachts. He looks like an old **sailor** with his cap and **pipe**. She sees that the boats have names painted on the side, like *Sea Horse, Mary Jane* and *The Jolly Roger.* How nice! she thinks and stands up to take a photo.

Just at that moment a man jumps from the deck of the

Cornwall ist der südwestlichste Landesteil Englands und ein beliebtes Urlaubsziel. Raue, steile Felsen, die sich mit langen Stränden und malerischen Buchten (Engl. **cove**) abwechseln, prägen die Küstenlandschaft.

Jolly Roger and **runs past** Anne Sophie. He is carrying a large bag which **bumps** her leg. It makes a sound like metal and it hurts.

"Ouch! Hey, watch where you're going!" Anne Sophie shouts.

The Jolly Roger	Totenkopfflagge, *wörtl.*: der fröhliche Roger
to run past	vorbeirennen
to bump	anrempeln
in his mid-40s	Mitte vierzig
⚡ Aye, aye!	Jawohl! Zu Befehl!

But the man doesn't stop running.

Anne Sophie finishes her postcard and starts to leave. She walks past the old sailor, who is still working hard. A red sports car drives into the harbour car park. A man **in his mid-40s** gets out of the car. He is wearing expensive sailing clothes and sunglasses.

"Hey, George! Is my boat ready?" he shouts to the old sailor.

"**Aye, aye**, Mr Hartley. I checked it this morning."

Exercise 1: Opposites. Wie lautet das Gegenteil der folgenden Adjektive?

1. small _____*large*_____

2. peaceful _____

3. friendly _____

4. cheap _____

At 7 p.m. on the same day, Jake Smith is sailing out to sea. He likes fishing in the evening when the tourist boats are

mainland England	das englische Festland
in the distance	in der Ferne
binoculars *pl*	Fernglas
coastguard	Küstenwache
to capsize	kentern
lifeboat	Rettungsboot
to set	*hier:* untergehen

gone. He sails round Land's End, the most westerly point of mainland England, and away from the coast. After a while he sees something in the distance. He picks up his binoculars and sees a yacht that is lying on its side. Its big white sail is lying in the water. He sails closer.

"Hello! Are you alright? Is anyone there?" he shouts.

But there is no answer. Jake takes out his mobile phone. [i]

"Land's End Coastguard Station, McGregor here!"

"It's Jake Smith here. I have found a yacht in trouble. It has capsized."

"OK, Jake, tell me where you are and we will come quickly in the lifeboat."

Jake waits by the capsized yacht. He smokes a cigarette and watches the sun setting over the sea. Soon he hears the lifeboat coming. It's getting dark now. Liam McGregor, the coastguard rescue officer, takes out his torch. He searches the boat, but there is no one there.

"Help me lift the sail out of the water," he says to his partner, Sam Nolan.

The two men move over to the other side of the boat

Im Englischen wird das Wort **handy** nur als Adjektiv verwendet (praktisch, handlich) und nicht als Bezeichnung für ein Mobiltelefon (*mobile phone*).

and lift the heavy sail. Under it they find a body in the water.

"Good God, I know him!" shouts Jake in shock.

Exercise 2: True or false? Welche Aussagen sind korrekt? Markieren Sie mit richtig ✓ oder falsch – !

1. Jake likes fishing when it is quiet. ❒
2. He sees something far away. ❒
3. He calls the police. ❒
4. Liam McGregor works alone. ❒
5. Jake reads a book while he is waiting. ❒

It's breakfast time at the Sea View B&B 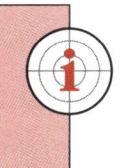 at Sennen Cove. Mrs Smith, the **landlady**, is carrying tea and toast into the dining room.

Als **Bed and Breakfast** (kurz: *B&B*) bezeichnet man eine Unterkunft bei Privatleuten, in deren Preis immer ein warmes Frühstück enthalten ist.

"Did you hear about the sailing **accident**?" she asks the Barbers. "It was on the local radio news this morning. Last night a yacht capsized and a man died. My husband found his boat."

rescue officer	Rettungshelfer(in)
torch	Taschenlampe
body	*hier*: Leiche
landlady	Wirtin
accident	Unglück
terrible	furchtbar
to move	*hier*: umziehen
to go into business	ein Geschäft gründen

"How **terrible**!" says Mrs Barber. "Was it a tourist?"

"No, he was called Roger Hartley. He lived here as a boy. But he **moved** to London as a young man and **went into business**. They say he was very rich!"

"How did the accident happen?" asks Mr Barber.

yet	schon, bis jetzt
strange	*hier*: merkwürdig, seltsam
surprised	überrascht

"No one knows that **yet**. It's very **strange**," says Mrs Smith. "Roger was a good sailor. I can't understand it! It really is terrible!"

Exercise 3: Choose the correct alternative. Lesen Sie weiter und wählen Sie das richtige Wort!

"Roger Hartley?" Anne Sophie repeat / repeats . "Was his boat called *The Jolly Roger*?"

"Yes! How did you know that?" asks Mrs Smith **surprised**.

Anne Sophie tells / tell the Barbers what she saw at the harbour the day before.

"I think you should tells / tell that to the police!" says Mr Barber.

"Mrs Smith, where is / are the nearest police station?"

"In Penzance," the landlady replies.

"OK. Anne Sophie, got / get your bag. I'm driving you to Penzance!"

Fishing for Clues

Detective Inspector Jack O'Reilly is sitting at his desk at the Penzance Police Station.

"OK, so you saw a man running from the yacht," the inspector says.

Anne Sophie nods.

"What did he look like?"

"He was quite tall and slim. He was wearing(i) jeans and a jacket

to nod	nicken
slim	schlank
hood	Kapuze
suspicious	verdächtig
forensic officer	Gerichts-mediziner
keel	Kiel

with a hood. I didn't see his face. It happened so fast."

"Did you see anything else suspicious?"

"Yes. He had a big bag and it hit me when he ran past. There was something made from metal inside it."

At that moment Inspector O'Reilly's mobile phone rings.

"Excuse me," he says, and he goes out of the room to take the call.

"Jack, it's Brendan here," the police forensic officer says. "We have found something interesting. We think someone took a piece off the keel of the boat."

"Brendan, you know I'm not an expert sailor. Can you explain it to me simply?"

> Um zu beschreiben was in dem Moment gerade war als etwas anderes passier-te, verwendet man das **Past Progressive.** Es wird mit *was/were* plus *-ing Form* gebildet.

Exercise 4: Correct the mistakes. Lesen Sie weiter und korrigieren Sie die sechs Fehler!

"Haha, Jack! Your the only man in Cornwall who doesn't like boats."
"Firstly, I'm from Dublin, as you know. And secondly, I get **seasick** if I just look at a boat. Just say me, Brendan."
"OK, the keel is the part that keeps a boat stable in the water. If you **damage** him, the boat is no longer stable. It can capsize easy."
How interesting, O'Reilly things. So maybe that german girl is a **witness** to a **crime**!

1. _____ 2. _____

3. _____ 4. _____

5. _____ 6. _____

Later that morning an **elderly** man and woman come into O'Reilly's office. The man looks **angry** and the woman is crying.

seasick	seekrank
to damage	beschädigen
witness	Zeugin
crime	Verbrechen
elderly	ältere(r/s)
angry	wütend

"Mr and Mrs Hartley, thank you for coming back. I know this is very hard for both of you. But I must ask you a few more questions about your son," the inspector says.

"We identified him 4 hours ago and the story is already in the newspapers!" Mr Hartley says angrily.

"Yes, I'm afraid bad news[i] travels fast," O'Reilly replies.

"Was it an accident?" Hartley's father asks.

Das Wort **news** (Nachrichten, Neuigkeiten) verlangt im Englischen immer ein Verb im Singular, obwohl es wie ein Substantiv im Plural aussieht.

"We are not sure. Did Roger have any problems?"

"No idea! He didn't talk to us much. He only came here to sail his boat," says Mr Hartley bitterly.

"Or did he have any enemies?" O'Reilly asks.

"Yes, lots. You can start with the neighbours. The Jones's boy hated Roger. He was jealous of him."

"Jones...?"

"Yes, Philip Jones. He was at school with Roger," says Mrs Hartley. "After school, they wanted to start a business together. But Philip isn't any good at business things. So Roger went to Surrey and started a company with

bad news travels fast	schlechte Nachrichten verbreiten sich schnell
enemy	Feind
to hate	hassen
jealous	neidisch
instead	stattdessen
married	verheiratet
divorced	geschieden
glad	froh

Giles Hill instead – 'Hartley and Hill'. They produce electronic parts for the computer industry."

"What about Roger's personal life? Was he married?"

"He was. And divorced – and a terrible divorce it was, too. Sheila lives in Canada now with her new husband. I'm glad she's gone."

O'Reilly writes in his notebook: Philip Jones, the jealous school friend; Giles Hill, the business partner; Sheila, the ex-wife. Very interesting, he thinks. But first I should go to the harbour and **check out** Anne Sophie's story.

Exercise 5: Match up the phrases. Welche der folgenden Satzteile gehören zusammen? Ordnen Sie zu!

1. [d] The elderly couple **a)** were not happily married.
2. [ ] Philip Jones is not **b)** make parts for computers.
3. [ ] 'Hartley and Hill' **c)** a good businessman.
4. [ ] Roger and Sheila **d)** identify their dead son.

In a small **terraced house** in Penzance, Philip Jones sits down on his sofa and puts his feet on the table. He opens a **can** of beer and picks up the local newspaper. When he reads the **headline,** 'Local man **drowns** in **freak** sailing accident', he has a big smile across his face.

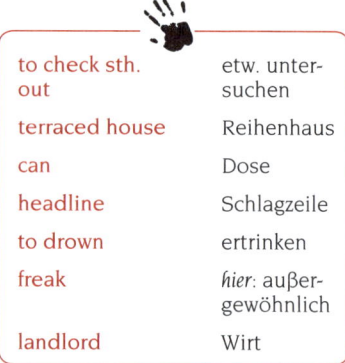

to check sth. out	etw. untersuchen
terraced house	Reihenhaus
can	Dose
headline	Schlagzeile
to drown	ertrinken
freak	*hier*: außergewöhnlich
landlord	Wirt

O'Reilly parks in the harbour car park next to the Sailor's Safety pub in Sennen Cove. There is a lot of noise and shouting inside the pub. Suddenly the door opens and a young man falls out onto the street.

"And don't come back until you can pay for your beer!" the **landlord** shouts after him angrily.

The man staggers away towards the harbour and O'Reilly follows him. In the harbour, he sees an old man wearing a sailor's cap. He is cleaning one of the yachts. The young man speaks to him.

"Not a penny[i] more! Go home and get some sleep until you're sober!" the old sailor shouts, and the other

> Der **penny** ist der hundertstel Bruchteil des britischen Pfunds. Die Mehrzahl ist **pence** (Abkürzung – "p").
> *The apple costs 90p.*

man staggers away without saying a word.

"Good afternoon, I'm Inspector O'Reilly from the Devon and Cornwall police. What's your name? Do you work here?"

"Yes, I clean the boats for the tourists. Everyone calls me Old George."

"Who was that young man who spoke to you?"

"That's just Clive, my good-for-nothing son. Drunk again!"

"I see. Were you here yesterday afternoon?" O'Reilly asks. Old George nods.

"Did you see Roger Hartley?"

"Yes, I did," Old George re-plies. "He sailed out to sea at around 4 o'clock. Lovely boat, the *Jolly Roger*! Hartley's dead now, isn't he? I read it in the newspaper."

to stagger	wanken, torkeln
sober	nüchtern
good-for-nothing	Taugenichts
drunk	betrunken
I'm afraid	Es tut mir leid, aber ...; leider

"Yes, I'm afraid he is. Did you see anything suspicious earlier in the afternoon?"

"No, it was very quiet all afternoon. There was no one here," Old George replies.

imagination	Fantasie
liar	Lügnerin
to have a fight	streiten
anything else	sonst noch etwas

"We have a witness. She saw a man running from the *Jolly Roger* at around 3 o'clock," O'Reilly replies.

"Oh yes, I remember. There was a young girl, about 17 or 18. But I didn't see a man. Young girls have a lot of imagination, you know. You can't believe everything they say."

But O'Reilly isn't so sure. He doesn't think that Anne Sophie is a liar.

"Well, I saw something strange two days ago," Old George tells the inspector. "I was at the pub over there, the Sailor's Safety. Hartley was outside in the beer garden with another man. They were having a fight."

"Do you know who the other man was?"

"Yes, it was Alan Walker, a Londoner. He keeps his boat here too, the *Mary Jane*."

Inspector O'Reilly's phone rings. "Sergeant Cole here, sir! I've got that telephone number you wanted for Giles Hill, Hartley's business partner."

"Thank you, Cole. I also want to find a Mr Alan Walker. He lives in London and he has a boat in Sennen Cove."

Der **Pub** ist im Vereinigten Königreich und Irland eine Kneipe und hat dort seinen festen Platz im sozialen Leben. Der Begriff leitet sich ab von "Public House", einem der Öffentlichkeit zugänglichen Haus.

"I'll see what I can do," answers Sergeant Cole.

"What about Philip Jones?" asks O'Reilly.

"I'm on my way to talk to him now, sir!" Cole replies.

"OK, that's all for now," O'Reilly says to Old George. "Here's my card. Phone me if you think of anything else."

Exercise 6: Pronouns. Ersetzen Sie die markierten Wörter durch die entsprechenden Pronomen!

1. O'Reilly doesn't think **Anne Sophie** is a liar.

   O'Reilly doesn't think **she** is a liar.

2. Did you see **Roger Hartley**?

   _____

3. **Hartley's parents** identify his body.

   _____

4. Walker keeps **his boat** at Sennen Cove.

   _____

5. Do you believe **Anne Sophie**?

   _____

O'Reilly gets in his car and dials Giles Hill's number.
"Hartley and Hill, Linda Jenkins speaking."
"Good afternoon, can I speak to Giles Hill, please?"
"I'm sorry, but Mr Hill is not in the office. He's on his way to Cornwall for a funeral. Mr

funeral	Beerdigung
excitedly	aufgeregt
to hang up	*hier*: auflegen

Hartley is dead, you know!" replies the secretary excitedly.
"No problem. I'll meet Mr Hill there," says O'Reilly and he hangs up.

Red Herrings

In a dark corner of the Queen's Head pub in Newquay, ⓘ Alan Walker sits alone at the bar. He is watching the local news on TV.

"This is Fred Cohen for the Nine O'Clock News. I'm standing outside the Penzance police station." At that moment a car arrives. The driver gets out and walks towards the **entrance** of the police station. The TV cameraman follows him and Cohen runs behind him with a microphone.

red herring	falsche Fährte
entrance	Eingang
rumour	Gerücht
path	Pfad, Weg
to appear	erscheinen
nosy	neugierig
nasty	gemein

"Inspector, there are **rumours** that Roger Hartley's death was not an accident. Do you have anything to say about that?"

"No comment at this time," O'Reilly says and walks away quickly.

I'm in big trouble now! thinks Walker. He drinks his double whisky and puts his head in his hands.

Newquay ist ein beliebter Ferienort an der Nordküste Cornwalls, etwa 40 Meilen von Sennen Cove entfernt. Die Stadt nennt sich selbst 'The Surfing Capital of Britain' und ist Austragungsort von Surfwettbewerben.

at   on   ~~onto~~   for   to   to

"Come on, Anne! I want to see the dead man's boat!"

"Me too, me too!" Little Jamie and his sister Louise are holding **1.** *onto* Anne Sophie's hands as they run along the path **2.** _____ the harbour.

"The boat isn't here now," Anne Sophie explains **3.** _____ the children. "The police are looking **4.** _____ it. Let's go for a walk **5.** _____ the beach instead."

Suddenly Old George appears behind them.

"What are you doing here?" he asks angrily.

"The children just want to look **6.** _____ the boats."

"Go away!" he shouts. "You are much too nosy!"

"Why is that man so nasty, Anne?" Louise asks.

"I don't know. But let's leave here quickly!"

Meanwhile in Penzance, Sergeant Cole rings the doorbell to a small terraced house. A middle-aged man opens the door. He is wearing old jeans and a dirty T-shirt.

"Mr Jones? I'm Sergeant Cole from the Penzance police. Can I come in?"

Jones shows Cole into the

| meanwhile | währenddessen |
| middle-aged | mittleren Alters |

living room. The room smells of cigarettes. There are pizza boxes and empty cans of beer on the table and on the floor.

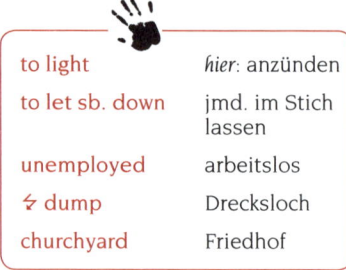

to light	*hier*: anzünden
to let sb. down	jmd. im Stich lassen
unemployed	arbeitslos
⚡ dump	Drecksloch
churchyard	Friedhof

"So what do you want?" Jones asks as he sits down and lights a cigarette.

"Did you know Roger Hartley?"

"Roger? Yes, he's dead, isn't he? I read it in the newspaper." Jones smiles.

"You don't seem very sad about that," says Cole.

"No, I'm not. Roger was my friend once. But he let me down. Look at Roger with his sports car and his big house. And look at me, unemployed and living in this dump!"

Exercise 8: Definitions. Vervollständigen Sie die Definitionen mit den angegebenen Wörtern!

dirty   nasty   nosy   angry   empty

1. A person who wants to know about other people's private lives is _____.

2. Someone who is aggressive or unfriendly is _____.

3. If you don't wash your clothes they are _____.

4. When you drink all the milk the bottle is _____.

5. If you shout because you are not happy about something, you are _____.

Friday morning is cold and rainy. Inspector O'Reilly is standing in the Sennen churchyard under a big umbrella. Next to him is Giles Hill. Old Mr and Mrs Hartley are talking to the vicar.[i] No one else is in the churchyard.

local man	Einheimischer
decision	Entscheidung
to cancel a contract	einen Vertrag kündigen
supplier	Lieferant
bankrupt	bankrott

"Hartley was a local man. Why aren't there more people here at his funeral?" O'Reilly asks Hill.

"Roger was not very popular, Inspector. To him business was important – friendship was not."

"Was he difficult to work with?"

"He sometimes made very hard decisions. Last April he cancelled a contract with one of our suppliers. That man is now completely bankrupt!"

"Really! Who do you mean?"

"A man called Alan Walker," replies Hill.

Alan Walker? I know that name, thinks O'Reilly. Old George told me about him. He had a fight with Hartley outside the pub. I must talk to him as soon as possible. But first I must finish with Hill.

"Do you have any other ideas? What about his private life?" asks O'Reilly.

"I think Roger was having women problems. I heard him on the telephone. He sounded very angry."

Ein **vicar** ist ein Gemeindepfarrer der *Church of England* (anglikanische Kirche). Das anglikanische Kirchenoberhaupt ist der jeweils regierende britische Monarch, also Königin Elisabeth II.

Exercise 9: Asking questions. Lesen Sie weiter und setzen Sie die Fragewörter richtig ein!

who   what   where   when

" **1.**   did this happen?" Inspector O'Reilly asks.

" **2.**   did he say?"

"It was a couple of weeks ago. He said, 'Leave me alone, you stupid woman. Don't phone here again!'"

"Charming! Do you think it was his ex-wife, Sheila?"

"No, she lives too far away. And I don't think Sheila and Roger were in contact anymore."

"OK, Mr Hill, I must ask you this question. **3.**   were you on Wednesday afternoon?"

"Sitting in a plane! I was on my way home from a business meeting in Chicago."

"I see. Do you have any idea **4.**   damaged Hartley's boat?"

"No, Inspector. I don't know anything about boats except that they make me seasick!" Hill says and he laughs.

"I understand," says O'Reilly with a smile. "I have the same problem. Thank you for your time, Mr Hill."

On the other side of the churchyard, O'Reilly sees Old George. He is watching the funeral from a distance and is smoking his pipe.

O'Reilly's mobile phone rings.

"Hello, it's Sergeant Cole here, sir! I've got an address for Alan Walker. His wife says he is on a golfing holiday in Newquay. I phoned him but he didn't answer. So I phoned the hotel. The receptionist said he checked

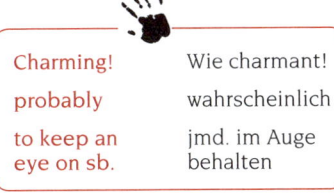

Charming!	Wie charmant!
probably	wahrscheinlich
to keep an eye on sb.	jmd. im Auge behalten

out an hour ago. He's **probably** on his way home now."

"Good work, Cole! What about your talk with Philip Jones?"

"Yes, I met him yesterday. He really hated Hartley."

"Where was Jones on Wednesday afternoon?"

"He says he was at home alone. He didn't leave the house all day."

"So he's got a motive and no alibi," O'Reilly replies.

"That's right, sir."

"You **keep an eye on him**. I'm going to talk to Alan Walker."

4 Old Friends

"Please sit down, Inspector. My husband should be home soon. Can I get you a cup of tea?"

"Yes, please, Mrs Walker."

She goes into the kitchen and O'Reilly looks around the living room. He sees some sailing trophies on a shelf. Mrs Walker comes back with the tea.

"Your husband is a keen sailor, isn't he?"

"Oh yes! He loves boats. He's an expert! Alan has his own yacht. He keeps it at Sennen Cove, next to Roger's boat."

shelf	Regal
keen	leidenschaftlich, eifrig
business associate	Geschäftspartner
to impress sb.	jmd. beeindrucken

She shows O'Reilly a photo of a man on board a yacht. On the side of the yacht is the name *Mary Jane*.

"That's my name, Inspector. Alan named the boat after me."

"Does your husband come from Cornwall, Mrs Walker?"

"No, he's a Londoner. But Roger taught him how to sail. Roger liked to take his business associates on board his yacht. He wanted to impress them!" she says bitterly.

"Is it true that your husband lost a lot of money because of Roger?" O'Reilly asks.

24

"Yes, it's a disaster. When Roger cancelled our contract, we lost everything. Now we **even** have to sell this beautiful house!"

Well, that's a strong motive,

even	sogar
to go for a run	joggen gehen
figure	Gestalt
shadow	Schatten
package	Paket

thinks O'Reilly. And Alan is an expert on yachts. Did he sabotage Hartley's boat?

Exercise 10: Opposites. Wie lautet das Gegenteil der folgenden Begriffe?

1. stand up _____

2. wife _____

3. won _____

4. hate _____

5. weak _____

"I'm **going** out **for a run**. The children are already in bed," Anne Sophie tells Mrs Barber that evening.

"Thanks, Anne! Don't be too late. Eric and I want to go to the pub later and we need you to babysit."

Anne Sophie runs along the beach. It's getting dark and the tourists and surfers have gone. At the ice cream kiosk she stops to have a rest. The kiosk has closed now. On the beach she sees two dark **figures** in the **shadows**, one tall and one short. The tall one gives a **package** to the other one. Then he turns and walks away. The short figure comes

scared	verängstigt
to hold one's breath	den Atem anhalten
to grab	greifen, fassen
several times	mehrmals
cruel	grausam
selfish	egoistisch
doorway	Türöffnung
at top speed	mit voller Geschwindigkeit

along the beach in Anne Sophie's direction.

She feels scared. She hides behind the ice cream kiosk and holds her breath. Suddenly a man's face looks round the corner of the kiosk.

"You again!" Old George shouts. "I warned you not to be so nosy," and he grabs her arm.

"Mrs Walker, did you know Roger Hartley personally?"

"Yes, Inspector, I met him several times. And his wife, Sheila."

"What happened between Hartley and Sheila?"

"Roger was a cruel, selfish man! Sheila left him and moved to Canada. I believe she is much happier[i] there."

"If you think of anything else, please call me. Here's my card and here's the number of the police station..."

Inspector O'Reilly hears a noise and looks up. A man is standing in the doorway.

"Alan Walker?" asks O'Reilly.

The man turns and runs out of the room. Quickly, O'Reilly follows him into the street. Walker

> Bei Adjektiven, die auf -y enden, wird in der Steigerung das -y durch ein i ersetzt. z.B.
> *happy, happier, happiest*

gets into his car and drives off at top speed. O'Reilly runs to his car and drives after him. He turns a corner and sees that the road ahead is empty.

Oh no, I've lost him! Where has he gone? he thinks.
But then he sees Walker's car parked on the other side of
the road. Walker is sitting behind the steering wheel with
his head in his hands.

Exercise 11: Contracted forms. Lesen Sie weiter und
ergänzen Sie die Kurzformen!

"Penzance Police Station, Sergeant Cole speaking. How
can I help you?"
"My **1.** name is _____*name's*_____ Eric Barber. **2.** I am
_____ phoning to report a missing person. Our au
pair, Anne Sophie Niedermair, has disappeared. She went
for a run and never came back."
"Anne Sophie? **3.** She is _____ a potential
witness in the Hartley case, **4.** is not _____
she? **5.** We will _____ treat this as a top priority!"

Walker sits on the back seat
of O'Reilly's car in handcuffs.
"You are our top suspect,
you know, Mr Walker. You
were in Cornwall all week.
You have a motive. And you
know how to sabotage a
yacht. All the evidence is
against you."

steering wheel	Lenkrad
to disappear	verschwinden
potential	möglich
case	Fall
to treat	behandeln
handcuffs *pl*	Handschellen
suspect	Verdächtiger
evidence	Beweis(mittel)
against	gegen

27

"I know! That's why I tried to run away. I panicked! But Inspector, you must believe me. I didn't sabotage that boat. I was very angry with Hartley, but I'm not a murderer."

"Why were you really in Cornwall?"

murderer	Mörder
to change one's mind	sich anders entschließen
to beg sb. for sth.	jmd. anflehen um
She didn't want me to know.	Sie wollte nicht, dass ich es erfahre.
to hit sb.	jmd. schlagen
right away	sofort

"I wanted to sail my yacht one last time! I have to sell the *Mary Jane*, Inspector. I'm bankrupt."

"A witness saw you fighting with Hartley outside the Sailor's Safety on Monday evening."

"Yes, that's true. Hartley was an arrogant pig! My wife called him two weeks ago. She tried to make him change his mind about the contract. She begged him for help. She didn't want me to know, but Hartley told me. He laughed about it. He thought it was funny. So I hit him! But I didn't kill him!"

"You knew Hartley's boat well, didn't you? Hartley took you sailing. Isn't that true?"

"Yes, the three of us had some good times together on the *Jolly Roger*."

"Three? Who was the third person?" asks O'Reilly.

"Giles, of course. He and Roger often went sailing together and sometimes I went with them."

"Giles Hill? He told me he gets seasick just by looking at a boat!" O'Reilly says in surprise.

"He said that?" Walker asks and he laughs.

Just then O'Reilly's phone rings. "Hello? Yes, Cole, what is it? Anne Sophie has disappeared? OK, I'll come back to Cornwall right away!"

Exercise 12: True or false? Welche Aussagen sind korrekt? Markieren Sie mit richtig ✔ oder falsch – !

1. Walker went to Cornwall to play golf. ☐
2. Walker lost all his money. ☐
3. O'Reilly thinks Walker could be the murderer. ☐
4. Giles Hill gets seasick on boats. ☐

5 The Net Tightens

Anne Sophie is **trapped** inside the cabin of a small boat in

to tighten	sich zusammenziehen, enger werden
trapped	gefangen
tied	gefesselt
tape	Klebeband
mess	Durcheinander
to get rid of sb.	jmd. loswerden
deal	Handel

Sennen Cove harbour. Her hands are **tied** behind her back and there is **tape** over her mouth. Old George and another man are sitting at a table on the other side of the cabin.

"What a **mess**!" says the younger man. "I only wanted **to get rid of** Roger, the pig!

Do you know, he tried to block my **deal** with the Americans. I told him that that was the best way to make money. But he didn't listen."

"I know, Mr Hill. Hartley never listened to anybody."

"But what are we going to do [1] with this girl now? She isn't part of our plan," Hill says nervously.

"How about another sailing accident, sir?"

> **going to + Infinitiv** bezieht sich auf die Zukunft. Es wird verwendet:
> a) um persönliche Pläne und Absichten für die Zukunft auszudrücken:
> *I'm going to drive to Paris next summer.*
> b) für Ereignisse in der Zukunft, die man als logische Folge einer Handlung ansieht.
> *Oh no, look! The cat is going to catch that bird!*

"Don't be stupid, George! The girl isn't a sailor. It must look like a swimming accident. We'll sail out towards the beach. Then we'll hit her on the head and throw her in the water. How's that for a plan."

"Aye, sir. That'll work."

Exercise 13: Choose the correct alternative. Lesen Sie weiter und wählen Sie das richtige Wort!

"Sergeant Cole here, sir. **1.** Where / Who are you now?"

"I'm turning onto the road to Sennen Cove. **2.** What are / What is the news on Anne Sophie?" O'Reilly asks.

"We had a call from a local woman. She was walking **3.** his / her dog near the beach. She saw two **4.** men / mens **dragging** a young woman in the direction of the harbour. She **5.** is thinking / thinks one of the men was Old George."

"Right. I'm on my way," O'Reilly replies.

He drives at top speed to the harbour, parks his car and runs towards the boat park. There is no one there except a young man, sitting alone on the harbour wall and drinking a can of beer.

| to drag | schleppen |
| to jump up | aufspringen |

"Hey, I know you," O'Reilly says. "You're Clive, Old George's son, aren't you?"

The young man **jumps up** and tries to run away. O'Reilly jumps up onto the harbour wall and grabs his arms.

"You're not going anywhere. You are under arrest."

"It wasn't my idea!" Clive shouts drunkenly.

"What do you mean? What was not your idea? Tell me everything you know," O'Reilly orders.

to be under arrest	verhaftet sein
drunkenly	betrunken
to order	befehlen
dirty work	Drecksarbeit
wave	Welle

"It was Mr Hill's idea. He wanted it to look like a sailing accident. He asked my father to organize it. I had to do the dirty work, as usual. But I need the money, Inspector!"

"Clive, are you talking about the *Jolly Roger*?" O'Reilly asks.

Clive nods his head.

"And where is your father now?"

"He just went out to sea in his motorboat."

"Where is he going? Is he alone?"

"No, there are two other people on board. They are going towards the beach," Clive replies.

O'Reilly takes out his mobile phone and rings the Coastguard Station.

Ten minutes later, Inspector O'Reilly is on board the lifeboat with the coastguards, Liam McGregor and Sam Nolan, sailing out to sea.

"The waves are quite high this evening. There is a storm coming," says Nolan.

"Are you alright, Inspector?" asks McGregor. "You look a bit green in the face."

"Don't **worry about** me. We must **catch** the other boat. Look over there! I think I can see them!" O'Reilly shouts.

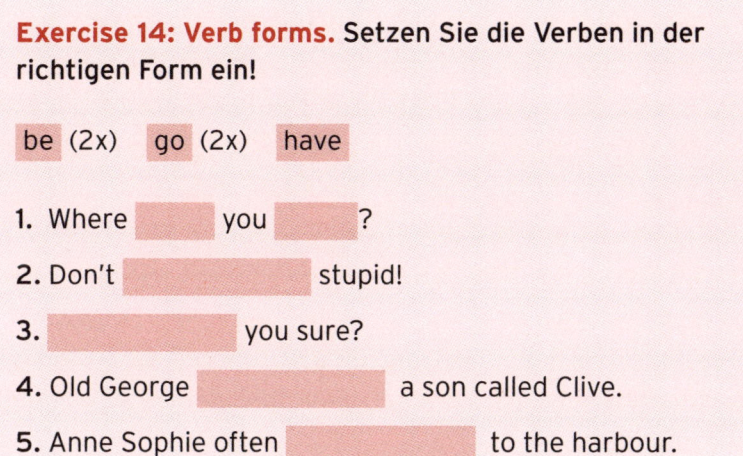

Exercise 14: Verb forms. Setzen Sie die Verben in der richtigen Form ein!

be (2x)　go (2x)　have

1. Where _____ you _____ ?
2. Don't _____ stupid!
3. _____ you sure?
4. Old George _____ a son called Clive.
5. Anne Sophie often _____ to the harbour.

On the deck of the motorboat, Hill and Old George are **preparing** to throw Anne Sophie overboard.

"**Untie** her hands," Hill says. "And take the tape off."

"Help, help! Someone help me!" Anne Sophie shouts as soon as her mouth is free.

"There's no one here to help you, my dear," says Old George with a nasty smile.

"Shut up, George. Listen! Can you hear something?" Hill asks.

"Just the wind, sir. There's a storm coming."

"No, listen! There's something else," Hill shouts nervously.

to worry about	sich Sorgen machen um
to catch	*hier*: einholen
to prepare	vorbereiten
to untie	losbinden
engine	Motor

They hear the sound of an **engine** in the distance.

33

to splash	schwappen
in despair	verzweifelt
life buoy	Rettungsboje

"Thank God! It's the lifeboat. Over here! Over here!" shouts Anne Sophie and waves [i] her arms.

"Damn! Forget the girl, George. Let's get out of here!"

Hill starts the engine and turns the boat away from the coast and out to sea.

"Can't you go any faster?" O'Reilly shouts at McGregor.

"Don't worry, sir. That little motorboat can't get far in bad weather like this."

"Faster, sir! They're getting closer," shouts Old George. Suddenly a big wave splashes over the side of the boat and the engine stops.

"It's all over, George. We're finished!" Hill says in despair.

Seconds later the lifeboat arrives. Nolan ties the two boats together. McGregor helps O'Reilly to go on board the motorboat.

"You two are under arrest for sabotaging Roger Hartley's boat and for kidnapping Anne Sophie Niedermair!" the inspector shouts as soon as he is on deck.

> Das englische Wort **wave** wird sowohl als Verb als auch als Substantiv verwendet, mit unterschiedlichen Bedeutungen. Das Verb **to wave** bedeutet „winken", während das Substantiv **wave** eine Welle bezeichnet.

McGregor helps him to handcuff the two men. "Now, where is she?"

"Look, there she is! In the water!" McGregor shouts. "The waves washed her overboard."

He grabs a life buoy and jumps into the water.

Anne Sophie is trying to stay **afloat** in the stormy sea. The waves are very high now, and her mouth and nose are full of salt water. McGregor

afloat	über Wasser
to cling onto	sich fest-klammern an
safety	Sicherheit

swims towards her as fast as he can. Suddenly a big wave hits her and she goes under. But McGregor gets to her just in time. He grabs her arm before she sinks. She **clings onto** the life buoy and McGregor swims with her back to **safety**.

Exercise 15: Hidden words. Finden Sie zehn Begriffe rund um Boote und Wassersport!

M	A	L	W	E	M	W	O	T	S
O	V	E	R	B	O	A	R	D	A
G	K	I	S	R	T	V	D	E	I
D	E	S	U	A	O	E	A	C	B
P	E	W	R	T	R	I	C	K	O
I	L	I	F	E	B	U	O	Y	T
L	E	M	I	N	O	T	U	Z	N
L	Y	T	S	E	A	S	I	C	K
O	R	E	T	S	T	M	A	B	E
D	E	A	K	Y	A	C	H	T	E

Two days later the sun is shining and the sea is calm. Anne Sophie is sitting in a deckchair in the garden of the B&B.

| deckchair | Liegestuhl |
| to look forward to sth. | sich auf etw. freuen |

"Here's a cup of tea for you, Anne," says Mrs Barber. "Is everything OK?"

"Yes, thank you. I'm fine," Anne Sophie replies.

She takes out her mobile phone to write a text message.

> Dear Mum and Dad, I am feeling much better now. I am looking forward to seeing you next week in Heidelberg. You won't believe how many exciting stories I have to tell you!

Murder in the Classroom

Lillian Flint

Death at the Desk

Constable Clive Ross and Inspector Ben Stephens are at the Whitechapel[i] police station in east London. Stephens is drinking a cup of tea. His large face is red, and his hair is also red. Ross is reading the newspaper. He is tall and has black hair. Their boss, Chief Inspector Elizabeth James, comes in. She is frowning.

Constable	Wachtmeister
Chief Inspector	Hauptkommissarin
to frown	die Stirn runzeln
primary school	Grundschule
to lean against sth.	lehnen an
headmistress	Schulleiterin

"A teacher is dead at Greenbell Academy." She gives Stephens a piece of paper. "Here's the address. Go now!"

The primary school Greenbell Academy is empty on a Friday afternoon. An ambulance is parked outside the school. Two men are leaning against it, smoking cigarettes. Constable Ross and Inspector Stephens walk into the school and see the headmistress, Mrs Reese, walking up and down the

Whitechapel liegt im Londoner East End, das schon immer ein besonders armer und rauer Stadtteil war. Der Serienkiller Jack the Ripper trieb in den 1880ern in Whitechapel sein Unwesen. Heute leben hier viele Einwanderer aus Bangladesch.

corridor. She is an attractive woman in her late fifties.

"Thank you for coming," she says breathlessly.

She opens the classroom door. A woman with long, dark hair is lying face down on the teacher's desk at the front of the classroom. It looks as if she is sleeping.

breathlessly	atemlos
desk	Schreibtisch
paramedic	Sanitäter
heart attack	Herzinfarkt
still	*hier*: trotzdem; noch
dreadful	furchtbar, schrecklich
to shake	zittern

Exercise 1: Odd one out. Welches Wort ist das „schwarze Schaf"? Unterstreichen Sie das Wort, das nicht in die Reihe passt!

1. teacher   primary school   ambulance   classroom

2. frown   pace   smile   laugh

3. headmistress   boss   Chief Inspector   secretary

4. ugly   good-looking   pretty   attractive

"The paramedics say it was a heart attack," says Mrs Reese.

"Yes, I know, but we still have to ask you some questions," Ross says and takes out a notepad. "Tell us what happened."

"She was cold when I found her. Oh God, it's just dreadful." Mrs Reese's hands are shaking. "Her name is Lynn Cooper."

"Do you know when it happened?" Ross asks.

"Between half past three and half past five."

"How do you know that, Mrs Reese?"

sweet wrapper	Bonbonpapier
evidence bag	Tüte für Beweise
It runs in the family.	Es liegt in der Familie.
fault	Fehler
surprised	überrascht
suddenly	plötzlich

The headmistress thinks for a moment. "Classes finish at half past three and I was busy until half past five. First I had a meeting with one of my teachers at four o'clock." "Is he or she still here?"

"No, Jonathan left at half past four. Then I did some work and didn't look at the clock again until half past five."

Stephens sees something under the desk and picks it up. It is a sweet wrapper and he puts it in an evidence bag.

"Before I go home I always walk through the school checking all the classrooms. And... that's when I found her," Reese says.

"She is very young to have a heart attack. Was she ill?" Ross asks.

"Both of Lynn's parents have heart problems. I think it runs in the family." Mrs Reese is crying. "She was a new teacher and I made her work too hard. It's all my fault."

"Mrs Reese, I know this is a shock for you," Stephens says.

"Yes, yes, it is. She is the second teacher to go this year."

The policemen look surprised.

"What happened to the first teacher?" Stephens asks.

"Megan Timms left suddenly."

"We are sorry. Mrs Reese, we would like you to come down

Both of bezieht sich immer auf zwei Personen bzw. Sachen und bedeutet „beide von ihnen". Das Gegenteil und die Verneinung wäre **neither of**, z.B. *Neither of them are coming.* Sie kommen beide nicht. Für mehr als zwei Personen/Sachen nimmt man **all of/none of**, z.B. *All/none of the pupils* know about it.

to the station to make a statement? Then you can tell us the whole story."

"Of course, of course," says Mrs Reese miserably.

statement	Aussage
miserably	traurig, niedergeschlagen
a dream come true	ein wahrgewordener Traum
pearl necklace	Perlenkette
worried	besorgt
I'm afraid ...	Es tut mir leid, aber ...; leider
note	Notiz; Zettel
PE (Physical Education)	Sportunterricht
to catch up	*hier*: etw. aufarbeiten
pupil	Schüler
bell	Glocke, Klingel
to ring	läuten

One week later, a new teacher, Anna Formella, arrives. Anna is tall, blonde and Canadian.

"I am so happy to start teaching at Greenbell, Mrs Reese. It really is a dream come true."

"Well, we are very happy you could start so spontaneously, Anna," Mrs Reese says. She is playing with her pearl necklace and seems worried.

"Can I speak with the last teacher of my class?" Anna asks. "I would like to talk to her about the children."

"I'm afraid that's not possible, but I can give you Lynn's notes. And Roberta can help you. She teaches PE and English. She has Lynn's class in room 101 right now."

"Thank you. I'm sure I will soon catch up," Anna says.

"You will meet the pupils after lunch."

The school bell rings for lunch[1] and children fill the corridor. Anna smiles at

In Großbritannien sind alle Schulen Ganztagsschulen und die Schüler essen in der Schule. Der Unterricht beginnt um ca. 8:45 Uhr und endet um ca. 15:30 Uhr. Danach gibt es für viele Schüler verschiedene AGs, Chorproben usw.

finally	endlich, schließlich
voice	Stimme
curly	lockig
gorgeous	herrlich
to taste	schmecken
horrible	schrecklich
sweet	süß
to scream	schreien

them. She feels very happy. She is **finally** living in her favourite city, and now she has a job, too. She feels so lucky.

"You must be Anna from Canada," says a deep **voice** behind her.

Anna turns around to see a tall man with **curly** brown hair and **gorgeous** blue eyes.

"Welcome," he says. "I'm Jonathan."

"Hi."

"And this is Roberta."

An athletic-looking young woman walks towards them.

"This is our new colleague, Anna," he says.

Roberta just looks at her. Anna smiles but Roberta takes Jonathan's arm and says, "Let's go to lunch, Jonathan."

"Come with us," Jonathan says to Anna.

The cafeteria is full of children and very loud. Anna, Jonathan and Roberta sit at the teachers' table. The cafeteria food is cold and **tastes horrible**, but Anna does not notice because Jonathan is smiling at her.

At half past one Anna meets her class. They are all eight or nine years old and very **sweet**. Only one girl, Shelley, is unfriendly.

"Miss Cooper," Shelley says quietly.

"What did you say?" Anna asks.

"Our teacher is dead!" Shelley **screams**.

Two other girls start crying.

Exercise 2: Present simple or present progressive?
Unterstreichen Sie die richtige Variante!

1. Mrs Reese often is staying / stays at school until six.
2. You can't speak to her now because she is making / makes a statement.
3. Classes normally are finishing / finish at half past three.
4. When the school bell rings, the children are going / go for lunch.
5. Today Anna is meeting / meets her pupils for the first time.

Frightened to Death

Ross reads the headline: "Teacher frightened to death!"
Stephens shakes his head. "Is Mrs Reese telling the truth?"

"I don't know," Ross says. "But something is definitely wrong at Greenbell."

"I don't understand – how can a young woman suddenly have a heart attack?" Stephens says.

Chief Inspector James comes into the room. "Stress," she says. "Stress can cause heart failure. Is that your report?"

He nods and she takes it from Stephens. "Where is the coroner's report, Ross?"

"The coroner is sending it over. But he says it was a heart attack," Stephens replies. "Nothing suspicious."

Ross holds up the newspaper. "The reporters love the story."

CI James shows them a letter. "This is from Mrs Reese's files. Remember the teacher

headline	Schlagzeile
frightened to death	zu Tode erschreckt
truth	Wahrheit
to cause	verursachen
heart failure	Herzversagen
report	Bericht
to nod	nicken
coroner	Gerichtsmediziner
suspicious	verdächtig
file	Akte
to remember	sich erinnern

before Lynn – the one who suddenly left Greenbell? Well,

her name is Megan Timms. Here's her **letter of resignation**." She puts it on the desk. Ross reads it out: "I cannot work here anymore. I am going home to Wales. Best wishes, Megan." CI James goes to the window

letter of resignation	Kündingungs-schreiben
rubbish	Müll
neighbour	Nachbarin
frizzy	gekräuselt
to shiver	zittern
to disappear	verschwinden

and looks out. It is grey and rainy and the streets are full of **rubbish**.

"One teacher leaves suddenly. One teacher dies. Something is wrong with that school. Ring[i] Megan Timms and find out what the problem was! And please do it now!"

At the weekend, Anna's **neighbour** Sally invites her in for a cup of tea. Sally is 35 years old, has **frizzy** red hair, and works from home as a journalist. She also has five cats. Anna loves cats and is happy to talk to someone so friendly.

As they sit drinking tea, Anna tells Sally about her new job in London.

Sally is surprised. "Greenbell? You're teaching at *the* Greenbell Academy? Don't you know the story? A

> **Telefonvokabular**
> **to ring sb. (up)** bedeutet „jmd. anrufen". Man kann auch sagen **to call/phone sb.** oder **to give sb. a call.** Wenn das Telefon klingelt, reagiert man mit **to answer/pick up the phone,** und „auflegen" übersetzt man mit **to put the phone down** oder **to hang up.**

teacher – frightened to death by her own class?"

Anna **shivers**. "Really?"

"She was the second teacher. The first one **disappeared**." That night, Anna cannot sleep.

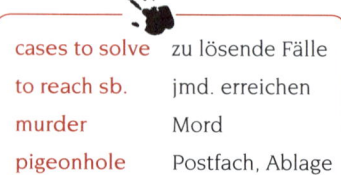

cases to solve	zu lösende Fälle
to reach sb.	jmd. erreichen
murder	Mord
pigeonhole	Postfach, Ablage

On a rainy Monday morning, Chief Inspector James is at work early. She has many files on her desk and many **cases to solve**. When Stephens arrives she asks, "What did Megan Timms say?"

"Nothing. I can't **reach her**."

The station phone rings and James answers. "London docks? Another one? Right away!"

CI James looks at Stephens. "Keep your coat on and go down to the docks. We have another **murder**."

East London is a busy place for crime.

That morning at school, Anna finds a note in her **pigeonhole**: One minus one = ?

She shows it to Jonathan and he laughs. "One of your pupils needs help with maths."

Exercise 3: Vocabulary pairs. Welche Wortpaare gehören zusammen? Ordnen Sie zu!

1. [c] tell   a) case
2. [ ] desk   b) pupil
3. [ ] newspaper   c) the truth
4. [ ] teacher   d) chair
5. [ ] solve   e) headline
6. [ ] homework   f) textbook

At lunch, Roberta and Anna eat rubbery fish and chips. Jonathan has soup because he is not feeling well.

"What happened to the teacher before Lynn?" Anna asks.

"Megan? She was mad," Roberta says. "We didn't like her, did we Jonathan?"

"Shut up, Roberta," Jonathan

rubbery	gummiartig
mad	verrückt
angry	ärgerlich, verärgert
female	weiblich
favourite	Lieblings-
drawer	Schublade
during	während
restless	unruhig
attention	Aufmerksamkeit
to giggle	kichern
I don't care!	Ist mir egal!

says and stands up to leave. "Bye Anna." His blue eyes look sad.

They watch him leave. Roberta is angry. "Be careful, Anna. Jonathan flirts with all of the female teachers."

Then the school bell rings and lunch is over. "Do you want to play badminton with me after school?" Roberta asks.

It is Anna's favourite sport.

"Only if I win," Anna says and they both laugh.

In the classroom Anna finds another note on her desk saying 'One minus one = ?' She puts the two notes in her desk drawer. During the lesson, the pupils are restless. Anna has to work hard to keep their attention. She asks for their English homework but Shelley does not have hers.

"Shelley, where is your homework?"

The girl does not look at Anna. The other pupils giggle.

"Shelley, I am speaking to you."

Shelley says, "I don't care."

"I will phone your mother," Anna says.
Shelley **shrugs her shoulders**.

After school, Anna goes to the **gym** to meet Roberta, but she isn't there. Then Anna hears loud voices coming from Roberta's **office** behind the gym. Suddenly Shelley runs out and past Anna. She is crying.

to shrug one's shoulders	die Schultern zucken
⚡ gym	Turnhalle
office	Büro
anyway	trotzdem
to forget	vergessen
to hide	sich verstecken

"Roberta?" Anna calls.
She walks across the gym and over to the office. The door is open but she knocks **anyway**.
"Oh hi," Roberta says. She looks tired and stressed. "I'm sorry, I **forgot** about badminton. I'm too tired to play today."
"Oh, okay. See you tomorrow, Roberta."
Anna turns around and leaves the gym. She does not see Shelley, who is **hiding** in a dark corner, watching her.

Exercise 4: True or false? Welche Aussagen sind korrekt? Markieren Sie mit richtig ✔ oder falsch – !

1. Anna's favourite sport is tennis. ☐
2. Anna finds a note in her pigeonhole at work. ☐
3. Jonathan is angry with Anna. ☐
4. The children cannot concentrate today. ☐
5. Anna puts the notes in her bag. ☐

 Sweet Poison

The next day, Anna finds two sweets on her desk. One red, one blue. Where do they come from? she wonders.

In class she works on adding and subtracting with the children.

Then little Shelley says: "One minus one equals none."

poison	Gift
sweets *pl*	Süßigkeiten
to wonder	sich fragen
strict	streng
to whisper	flüstern

Anna is surprised and takes out the notes from her desk. "Everyone, please look at page thirty in your maths books and do exercises one to three."

Exercise 5: Choose the correct alternative. Lesen Sie weiter und wählen Sie das richtige Wort!

Anna calls Shelley **1.** to / at her desk.

The other children are **2.** seeing / watching but Anna says "Get to work!" in a strict voice.

She whispers to Shelley, "Did you **3.** wrote / write these notes?"

"No," the girl **4.** tells / says .

Anna frowns **5.** at / to her. "Shelley...?"

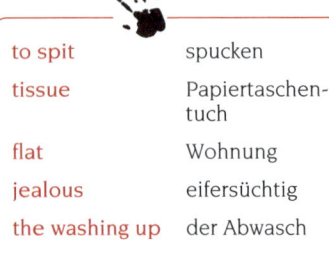

to spit	spucken
tissue	Papiertaschen-tuch
flat	Wohnung
jealous	eifersüchtig
the washing up	der Abwasch

"Yes, but..." Shelley starts crying.

A boy in class laughs at her and Shelley cries louder. Anna sees the sweets on her desk and gives one to the girl.

"Here, you can have the red one," Anna says.

Shelley takes the red one and then says: "No, wait. I want blue."

Shelley stops crying and eats the blue sweet. The other children watch. Anna eats the red one but it is too sweet. When no one is looking, she spits it out into a tissue and puts it in her pocket.

"Can we go on with the class now?" Anna asks.

Shelley smiles and nods her head.

That evening Anna goes to Jonathan's flat for the first time. They cook pasta together and later they open a bottle of wine and talk.

"Roberta thinks you are just a big flirt," Anna says.

He laughs. "Roberta is jealous."

Later, Anna helps with the washing up. In a kitchen drawer she finds photos of two young women.

"Who are they?" she asks.

Jonathan looks surprised, then angry.

"The teachers. The two teachers who have... gone."

Anna doesn't understand.

"The teachers before you," he says. His voice is aggressive.

"Why do you have their photos?"

Jonathan **takes a deep breath** and closes his eyes for a moment. Then he says: "Anna, please sit down."

Anna feels **afraid** as she sits down beside him. "What's wrong?"

Jonathan takes her hand. "When I was eighteen years old my first girlfriend died."

Anna is shocked. "How **terrible**."

"It was my fault. I was **drinking and driving**."

"She died in your car?"

"Yes," he says. He picks up the photos and looks at them. "And now Lynn and Megan are dead too."

He puts his head in his hands. "I just bring **bad luck** to everyone! Three beautiful girls are dead."

"But Lynn and Megan... that wasn't your fault."

He has tears in his eyes and doesn't look at Anna.

"Were those two teachers before me also your girlfriends?"

Jonathan doesn't say anything.

"Jonathan? Were they your girlfriends?"

He still has tears in his eyes when he says: "You shouldn't be here, Anna. You shouldn't be with me."

She **gives him a hug** and then

to take a deep breath	tief einatmen
to be afraid	Angst haben
terrible	schrecklich
drinking and driving	betrunken Auto fahren
bad luck	Pech
to give sb. a hug	jmd. umarmen

they watch television together in his living room.

When she stands up to go, he says, "Stay here tonight."

But she shakes her head and goes home at 10 p.m.

Exercise 6: Opposites. Wie lautet das Gegenteil der folgenden Verben?

1. to find   _to lose_
2. to sit down   _____
3. to stay   _____
4. to remember   _____
5. to laugh   _____

The next morning at 6:00 a.m., Anna is in her flat making her morning coffee when the phone rings. It is Mrs Reese.

"Anna, thank God you're there. I have terrible news."

Anna's heart starts beating hard. "What is it?"

"Your pupil Shelley…she's dead!"

Anna is so shocked she can hardly speak. "But…? What?! I don't understand!"

"Shelley died from poison. She died in her sleep last night." Anna is shaking.

"The school is closed today," Mrs Reese says. "I will ring you later. I need to be with her parents and the police now."

Anna feels cold. This is a nightmare. She knocks on her neighbour's door and wakes her up. Sally gives her a cup of tea and listens. Suddenly Anna remembers something and her eyes open wide.

"Oh my God! The sweets! Was it the sweets?"

to beat	schlagen, pochen
hardly	kaum
nightmare	Albtraum

Sally looks confused.

"You have to take me to the hospital, Sally. Right now!"

Two hours later, the doctor at the hospital has her test results. "You are 100% healthy," he tells Anna.

confused	verwirrt
exhausted	erschöpft
devastated	am Boden zerstört
criminal investigation	polizeiliche Ermittlung

"But a child died," Anna says. She starts to cry.

"Was she ill?" he asks.

"No, she was poisoned."

At noon Mrs Reese comes to Anna's flat. She looks exhausted and miserable.

"Shelley's parents are devastated," Mrs Reese says. "It is all so dreadful."

Mrs Reese asks Anna questions about Shelley's last day.

"There were two sweets on my desk. One red, one blue," Anna tells her.

"Oh my God! Did you eat one, too?" Mrs Reese asks.

Anna shakes her head. "I spat mine out. It was too sweet."

"Tell the police this when they come here. It's important. Even if it wasn't the sweets, tell them anyway."

Reese puts her hand on Anna's arm and says, "This is a criminal investigation. I think you should know that the police are also investigating Lynn's death. It's possible it wasn't a heart attack."

Mrs Reese closes her eyes. "It may be murder."

Anna's heart jumps. "What?"

"An inspector will visit you tomorrow. Anna, tell him everything you know."

A Deadly Sport

Chief Inspector James is drumming her fingers on the desk nervously while she waits for Ross.

As soon as he walks through the door, she asks, "So? What did the first teacher say?"

to move	*hier*: umziehen
vicar	Gemeindepfarrer
originally	ursprünglich
handwriting	Handschrift
Welsh	walisisch
missing persons report	Vermisstenanzeige

Ross is nervous and tired. "There's new information: Megan's parents died five years ago, and then she **moved** to London. I phoned the **vicar** in Bangor, in Wales, the town she **originally** came from. He thinks she is still teaching."

"Mrs Reese has a letter of resignation from Megan from ten months ago."

"It's not her **handwriting**. Someone tried to write like her!"

"Now that's interesting!" says his boss. "Did you phone the **Welsh** police?"

"Yes, and there's no **missing persons report**," Ross says.

> Es gibt keine Mehrzahl von **information**, im Gegensatz zum deutschen „Informationen". Folglich steht das Verb auch immer im Singular, z.B. *The information about the trip is very interesting.* Man übersetzt ‚eine Information' mit *a piece of* information.

"So basically she has disappeared but no one seems to know this?" the CI asks. "Go back to the school, Ross. Interview all of the teachers and the headmistress. Someone is lying."

Exercise 7: Forming questions. Unterstreichen Sie die richtige Variante!

1. Am I / I am healthy?
2. How did she died / die ?
3. Are the police investigated / investigating the murder?
4. Where did she originally comes / come from?
5. Are you going / Do you go to the hospital?

At 1:30 in the afternoon Anna is sitting on the sofa eating biscuits. The television is on, but she isn't really watching it. She can't seem to concentrate on anything and feels very frustrated. She has been at home for nearly a week now. What is going on at Greenbell? she wonders.

Jonathan calls and she nearly starts crying again. "Poor Shelley. Why did she die? How did she die?"

"It is very sad," Jonathan says. His voice is cold.

"Is that all you can say?"

"Anna, I'm sorry. I'm tired. See you tonight?"

"Okay, fine. Come over at eight."

She puts the phone down and the doorbell rings. It is Inspector Stephens. He has dark

| basically | eigentlich, im Grunde |
| to put the phone down | auflegen |

circles under his eyes and his face is red from the cold wind.

"Anna Formella?" He shows her his police badge. "May I come in?"

badge	Marke, Abzeichen
to act strangely	sich seltsam verhalten
out of the blue	aus heiterem Himmel
briefcase	Aktentasche
one's stomach is in knots	einen verkrampften Magen haben
seriously	ernsthaft, wirklich

Anna makes him a cup of tea and they sit at her kitchen table. He asks her many questions.

"Tell me about Shelley," he says. "How was she in class?"

"She often acted strangely."

"How?"

"She cried easily and sometimes said strange things out of the blue. She was not a good pupil."

Stephens takes some pieces of paper from his briefcase and puts them on the table.

"We found these in Lynn's desk and in her pigeonhole at the school," he says. "'One minus one = ?'."

Anna nods slowly. "Yes, Shelley said that once in class."

Ross puts three new notes on the table. The first note has Lynn's name on it in large, black letters. The second has Megan's name. The third has Anna's name.

Anna's eyes are wide open. She is scared and her stomach is in knots. Something is seriously wrong.

The inspector puts the letters back into his briefcase and frowns. "Are you friends with any of the teachers?"

"Yes, with Jonathan and Roberta."

Exercise 8: Translating adjectives. Ordnen Sie den
Adjektiven die passende Übersetzung zu!

1. ☐ unconcentrated   **a)** ernst

2. ☐ angry   **b)** verärgert

3. ☐ sad   **c)** verängstigt

4. ☐ scared   **d)** unkonzentriert

5. ☐ strange   **e)** traurig

6. ☐ serious   **f)** seltsam

"What about Megan Timms?" the inspector asks.

"I don't know her. She left the school before Lynn, then Lynn had a heart attack…"

Ross nods. "We are worried about your safety, Anna. Stay in your flat today and do not speak to anyone about this."

"I don't understand, Inspector."

"We will call you tomorrow. If anything suspicious happens, ring me." He gives her his business card.

safety	Sicherheit
business card	Visitenkarte
to meow	miauen

After Stephens leaves, Anna knocks on Sally's door but her neighbour is not home. The cats are meowing behind the door.

That evening Jonathan comes to Anna's flat for dinner. She has made pizza but there is only apple juice to drink.

"I'm sorry I can't give you something more interesting. I can't go shopping because I **am not allowed to** leave my flat."

"This will be over soon, Anna. Don't worry," he says.

Anna **notices** that Jonathan doesn't eat much dinner.

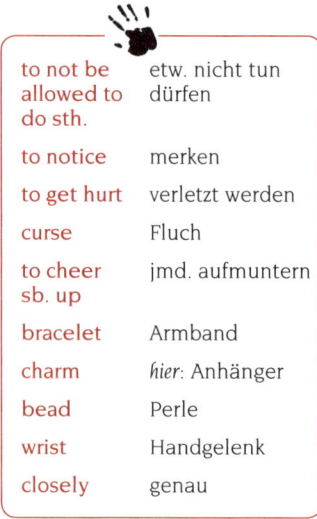

to not be allowed to do sth.	etw. nicht tun dürfen
to notice	merken
to get hurt	verletzt werden
curse	Fluch
to cheer sb. up	jmd. aufmuntern
bracelet	Armband
charm	*hier*: Anhänger
bead	Perle
wrist	Handgelenk
closely	genau

"Don't you like pizza?" she asks.

"I'm not hungry. Anna, listen to the police. Do whatever they tell you to do. Something is wrong at Greenbell and I don't want you to **get hurt**."

"What do you mean?"

"It's a **curse**," he says.

Anna starts crying. "I love being a teacher and I was so happy to get the job at Greenbell, but nothing is going right. A young girl is dead and now you are talking about curses?"

Jonathan holds her hand. "I know what will **cheer you up**."

He gives her a small white box. She finds a **bracelet** inside with little silver **charms** and pink **beads**.

"It's beautiful," she says.

Jonathan smiles and puts it on her **wrist**. "I really like you, Anna."

She looks **closely** at the bracelet. There are three little charms: a tennis ball, a cat, and a flower.

"I like you too," she says.

They kiss and Anna has **butterflies** in her stomach.

But a moment later, Jonathan suddenly stands up. "I should go. School is opening again tomorrow."

butterfly	Schmetterling
bored	gelangweilt
to hope	hoffen
headache	Kopfschmerzen

"What? Nobody told me. What about my pupils?"

"Anna, you have to stay at home. The police said 'don't leave your flat'."

He hugs her. "Good night. Let's speak tomorrow."

He kisses her and, for a moment, she forgets her problems.

Exercise 9: English and German. Lesen Sie weiter und vervollständigen Sie den Text mit den angegebenen Wörtern!

during   ~~day~~   biscuits   calling   attention

ring   answer

The next **1.** *day* Anna is still sitting on the sofa at home, eating **2.** and not paying **3.** to what is on the television. She is **bored** and really wants to know what is going on. **4.** the lunch break she **hopes** Jonathan will **5.** , but he doesn't. She doesn't hear anything from the police either. She tries **6.** Mrs Reese, but there is no **7.** .

Anna has a **headache**. Why is no one telling her what is going on? Anna makes a decision: she will leave her flat

to sneak	schleichen
school grounds	Schulgelände
ground floor	Erdgeschoss
to get into trouble	Schwierigkeiten bekommen
to tiptoe	auf Zehenspitzen schleichen
locker room	Umkleide
footsteps *pl*	Schritte

and go to the school. She cannot wait any longer.

At quarter to two the pupils are in class and Anna **sneaks** into the **school grounds**. Her classroom is on the **ground floor** and she looks through the window. She sees that Roberta is teaching her class. Roberta is shouting at the children. The children are standing beside their desks and they look afraid. Shelley's desk is gone.

Then Roberta turns to the window. Does she see Anna? Anna quickly hides in the bushes. She does not want anyone to see her – she could **get into trouble**. But why are the children afraid? Anna has a strange feeling in her stomach. She goes into the school. The classroom doors are shut but Mrs Reese's office door is open a little. Anna **tiptoes** down the corridor to the gym.

Roberta's room is at the back of the gym. The door is unlocked. There is a desk in the office and Anna opens the drawers. She finds a bag of sweets – the same sweets that Shelley ate. There is also a small glass bottle. Then Anna hears someone coming. She *must* hide!

Anna quickly opens a second door at the back of the room. It is a very large **locker room**. She closes the door behind her and looks for the light switch but cannot find it. She uses her mobile phone as a light.

Suddenly Anna hears **footsteps**. She runs to the back wall.

There are footballs, tennis rackets and nets along the wall, and she tries to hide in the shadows. Then she sees it: a trap door in the floor of the locker room.

racket	Schläger
shadow	Schatten
trap door	Falltür
smell	Geruch
cellar	Keller
to crouch	sich niederkauern
outline	Umriss

The footsteps are louder now. Anna opens the trap door and suddenly there is a terrible smell. There are stairs going down into the darkness. Is it a cellar? Anna wonders.

The footsteps are very close now – just outside the room. Quickly, she goes down the stairs. Someone is opening the door to the room. Anna stops, crouches down on the stairs and looks back to see who is coming in. She sees the outline of someone entering the room, but she cannot see their face. It is too dark.

Exercise 10: Unscramble the text. Lesen Sie weiter und bringen Sie die Sätze in die richtige Reihenfolge!

a) Anna shines the light from her mobile phone on to the stairs as she walks further down.
b) "Who's there?" the man asks.
c) "Hello?" a man's voice says.
d) Anna stays very still but she cannot breathe – the terrible smell from the bottom of the stairs is so strong.

1	2	3	4

shiny	glänzend
to lose one's balance	das Gleichgewicht verlieren
unconscious	bewusstlos
fire exit	Notausgang

"Hey!" the voice calls.

Anna sees something shiny at the bottom of the stairs. It is a charm bracelet – the same kind Jonathan gave her. It is on the arm of the body of a woman, who is clearly very dead. Anna screams and screams. She loses her balance and falls down the stairs, landing on the dead woman. For Anna, everything goes black.

Mrs Reese hears the screams from her office and runs into the gym to find Jonathan and Roberta.

"What was that noise?" Mrs Reese says. "Why aren't you in your classrooms?"

They don't answer. Jonathan goes into Roberta's office and Mrs Reese follows. They find the open trap door in the locker room. They look down the stairs and see Anna at the bottom of the stairs. She is unconscious.

"Anna!" Mrs Reese screams, panicked.

"Call the ambulance!" Jonathan says.

When Mrs Reese puts the phone down, she sees something else. There is another person at the bottom of the stairs with Anna. Mrs Reese tries not to scream again.

In the gym, Roberta is hiding in a dark corner. She watches Jonathan leave the gym through the fire exit doors. Then Roberta walks quietly into her office. She takes a few things from her desk drawer, puts them in her bag and leaves the gym. The sirens of the ambulance get louder.

The Terrible Truth

In hospital, Anna wakes up with Jonathan by her side. He is holding her hand.

"What happened?" she asks.

"You are the one for me," Jonathan says. "I will protect you, Anna." He touches her charm bracelet.

"What happened?" Anna says again.

She rubs her head and feels a large lump. She tries to remember what happened but doesn't remember anything. Just then Police Constable Ross and Inspector Stephens walk into the room.

He holds up a charm brace-

to protect	beschützen
lump	Beule
to be under arrest	verhaftet sein
to rush	hasten, sausen
Don't you dare!	Wag(t) es bloß nicht.

let and walks towards Jonathan. "Jonathan Shurefire," Ross says. "You are under arrest…"

Anna is so shocked that she cannot breathe. Suddenly the door flies open. Roberta rushes in and pulls Jonathan away from Anna's bed.

"Get back," she screams and pushes Jonathan into a corner. She stands in front of him, blocking him from the police. Then she pulls a knife out and points it at the policemen.

"Don't you dare touch him!" she screams.

over and over	immer wieder
tears *pl*	Tränen
to tremble	zittern
to stab	(zu)stechen

Stephens wants to stop her but Ross says, "Wait."

Anna stares at the scene with eyes wide open.

Jonathan is whispering to Roberta but he looks scared.

"Don't hurt him, please!" Anna screams.

Roberta laughs. "Anna, he has hurt me over and over. He'll hurt you, too."

She turns to Jonathan. "You broke my heart."

"Roberta, let me explain," Jonathan says.

"No! It's too late," Roberta screams as tears roll down her face. "All of those other girls, but never me. You loved their attention. First Megan. Then Lynn. But never me."

"No," he says quietly. "Not you."

"Then Anna came and you gave her a bracelet, too."

Roberta spits at Anna. Anna is so frightened that she is trembling all over.

"You're finally mine, Jonathan," Roberta says.

"Roberta Jones, put the knife down and let's talk about this," Ross says.

He walks over to her, but Roberta screams at him, "Get away!"

She pulls her hand back and high above her head. The knife shines in the light.

"Roberta," Anna says. "Please, Roberta."

Jonathan is looking at Anna and does not see the knife. The men rush in, but Roberta is so fast. She brings the knife down and stabs Jonathan in the chest.

Anna screams as he falls to the ground. Ross pushes the emergency buzzer, while Stephens pushes Roberta to the ground.

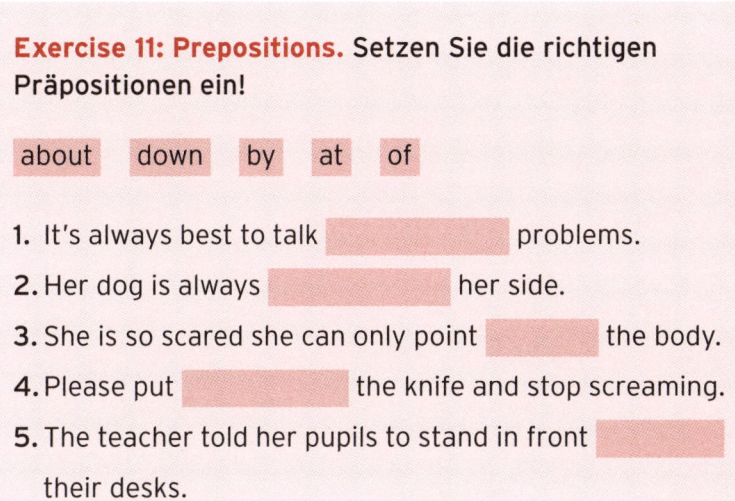

Exercise 11: Prepositions. Setzen Sie die richtigen Präpositionen ein!

about　　down　　by　　at　　of

1. It's always best to talk 　　　　　　 problems.
2. Her dog is always 　　　　　　 her side.
3. She is so scared she can only point 　　　　 the body.
4. Please put 　　　　　　 the knife and stop screaming.
5. The teacher told her pupils to stand in front 　　　　 their desks.

A glass bottle falls out of Roberta's pocket and rolls across the floor. Ross picks it up and reads the label. It is poison. Stephens puts Roberta in handcuffs. A few seconds later a nurse comes running into the room.

"Roberta Jones, you are under arrest for the deaths of Lynn Cooper, Megan Timms, Shelley Mansfield and the attempted murder of Jonathan Shurefire," Stephens says.

emergency buzzer	Notfallknopf
label	Etikett
handcuffs *pl*	Handschellen
attempted murder	versuchter Mord

They lead her out as the nurse runs for a doctor, but Anna can see that it's too late.

Jonathan is already dead.

Exercise 12: Questions and answers. Ergänzen Sie das richtige Fragewort und beantworten Sie dann die Fragen!

Where   what   ~~who~~   when   why

1.   *Who*   does Ross arrest first?

   _____

2.   _____   can Anna remember?

   _____

3.   _____   does the nurse arrive?

   _____

4.   _____   does Roberta want to kill Jonathan?

   _____

5.   _____   is the body of Megan Timms?

   _____

A Wedding to Die For

Caroline Simpson

1 The Perfect Wedding?

I'm here at last, Abigail thinks. It was a long journey from Liverpool to the Cotswolds.[i]

She drives up to the Manor House Hotel, a beautiful old building, and parks her car.

"This way, madam," says a pretty, young waitress.

She takes Abigail to a garden behind the house. Here the other guests are talking and drinking champagne.

at last	endlich
journey	Reise
wedding	Hochzeit
middle-aged	mittleren Alters
to remember	sich erinnern an

How romantic, thinks Abigail. A wedding in a rose garden.

"Hello Abigail, my dear," says a middle-aged woman who is wearing a large hat. "How lovely to see you again."

"Hello, Mrs Blenkinsop. I couldn't miss my old friend's wedding," Abigail replies.

"Sylvia will be so happy. Rupert, you remember Abigail, don't you?" Mrs Blenkinsop asks, turning around. "She was at school with Sylvia."

"Yes, of course. Our little

Die **Cotswolds** sind eine malerisch hügelige Region in Mittelengland, die mitunter auch als das Herz Englands bezeichnet wird. 1966 wurden die Cotswold Hills als **Area of Outstanding Natural Beauty** (Gebiet von außerordentlicher natürlicher Schönheit) klassifiziert.

Sherlock!" replies a man in a **suit** and smiles at Abigail. "How are you, my dear? Are you still **fighting crime**?"

"Hello, Mr Blenkinsop. I'm fine, thank you. And don't worry, I'm not here to **arrest** anyone!" Abigail laughs.

"Abigail, meet Trevor, my new **son-in-law**," says Mrs Blenkinsop.

Exercise 1: Adjectives and adverbs. Lesen Sie weiter und unterstreichen Sie die richtige Variante!

Trevor is an **1.** attractive / attractively young man with **2.** dark / darkly hair and blue eyes. He smiles **3.** warm / warmly and shakes Abigail's hand.

"Would you like a glass of champagne?" he asks **4.** polite / politely .

"I'm afraid there's no time for that now," says Mrs Blenkinsop. "Rupert, go and get Sylvia."

Rupert leaves **5.** quick / quickly .

The guests sit down. Minutes later Mr Blenkinsop comes back with his daughter. Sylvia is wearing a long, white wedding dress and there are roses in her hair. The band begins to play the Wedding March. Sylvia smiles happily as her father **leads** her towards the altar.

suit	Anzug
to fight	bekämpfen
crime	Verbrechen
to arrest	festnehmen
son-in-law	Schwiegersohn
to lead	führen

Later that afternoon, Abigail is sitting in the dining room.

delicious	köstlich, lecker
to wink	zwinkern
to pour	einschenken
only child	Einzelkind
accident	Unfall
bad luck	Pech

"I must say, this champagne is really delicious," says the man sitting on her left. "And the waitresses, too!" he jokes, winking at the pretty, young woman who is pouring champagne into his glass.

He is wearing a colourful shirt but no tie. He has a silver earring in one ear and a chain round his neck.

"I'm Stuart, Trevor's friend from London," he tells Abigail.

"Nice to meet you. Tell me something, Stuart. Sylvia's whole family are here: her parents, her sister, aunts, uncles, cousins...but where is Trevor's family?" asks Abigail.

"Trevor doesn't have any family. He is an only child and his parents died last year in a car accident. He has had a lot of bad luck in his life. But I must say, with Sylvia he is very lucky. ⓘ This wedding must cost a lot of money!"

"Yes, that's true. The Blenkinsops are a rich family," says the man sitting on Abigail's right. He is wearing a grey suit and thick glasses. "Abigail, you don't remember me, do you? It's Philip, Philip Morrison. I was in the same class as you and Sylvia at high school."

lucky and happy werden beide mit "glücklich" übersetzt, beschreiben aber unterschiedliche Aspekte von Glück:

lucky   Glück haben, z.B. wenn man im Lotto gewinnt

happy   glücklich sein, sich freuen, z.B. wenn man einen netten Abend mit guten Freunden verbringt.

"Oh, yes, of course!" Abigail replies. "Philip, I didn't know you were still in contact with Sylvia."

"I'm an accountant, you know. I work for Sylvia's parents. I manage their company's finances."

"That's interesting. Tell me a bit about their company. Sylvia never talked about business when we were young."

"Well, they import high quality French furniture from Alsace. It's very popular here and business is booming. Mr and Mrs Blenkinsop want to retire in a year or two. Then Sylvia and Trevor will manage the company together." Philip shakes his head sadly.

"Lucky old Trevor!" laughs Stuart Shields. "I must go and congratulate him."

He walks to the main table and whispers something in Trevor's ear. Then he leaves the dining room. Minutes later, Trevor gets up and follows him.

I should relax. I'm not on duty now, thinks Abigail.

She loves her job as Detective Inspector at the Liverpool Constabulary. But she sometimes finds it hard to stop working.

accountant	Buchhalter
company	Firma, Unternehmen
furniture	Möbel
Alsace	Elsass
to retire	in Rente gehen
to whisper	flüstern
on duty	im Dienst
Constabulary	Polizeibezirk

When Stuart comes back ten minutes later, Abigail sees that the pupils of his eyes are very large and his laugh is louder than ever.

Exercise 2: Happy or lucky? Setzen Sie die richtige Variante von „glücklich" ein!

1. Sylvia looks very *happy* on her wedding day.
2. I'm very _____ to see you!
3. Trevor, you're a _____ man to have a **wife** like Sylvia.
4. I nearly had an accident. But I was very _____ and the car missed me.
5. Thirteen is my _____ number.

Abigail is washing her hands in the **ladies' cloakroom** when the door opens and Sylvia comes in.

ladies' cloakroom	Damentoilette
wife	Ehefrau
bride	Braut
to hug	sich umarmen
to keep a secret	ein Geheimnis bewahren
pregnant	schwanger
yet	schon
to pass	vorbeigehen
⚡ the gents	Herrentoilette

"It's so lovely to see you!" says the **bride** and the two women **hug**.

"You look so beautiful today, Sylvia. And so happy."

"Abi, can you **keep a secret**? I'm **pregnant**! No one knows **yet**. I want to tell Trevor tonight, on our wedding night."

Half an hour later, Abigail is smoking a cigarette in the garden. On her way back to the dining room she **passes** the **gents** just as Trevor comes out. His eyes are wild and he has a big smile on his face.

When he sees Abigail, he quickly puts a small plastic packet in his suit pocket.

"Hey, great party, isn't it?" he laughs loudly. "The food is fantastic. I must go and congratulate the cook."

Abigail watches him leave. Poor Sylvia, she thinks.

The five-course dinner is finally over, and the band starts playing 'True Love'.

"Come on, darling," says Sylvia to Trevor. "It's time for the first waltz."

She leads him to the dance floor and the guests applaud loudly. After the waltz the lights go on and a waiter walks in. He is pushing a

trolley	Servierwagen
chef	Koch
to serve	servieren
To the happy couple!	Auf das Brautpaar!
bridesmaid	Brautjungfer
terrible	furchtbar
drunk	betrunken

trolley with the large wedding cake. Behind him comes the chef, wearing a tall white hat, and two waitresses with more champagne.

"What a beautiful cake. Well done, Mr Craddock!" says Mrs Blenkinsop.

"Thank you, madam," replies the chef, smiling. "I designed it myself, and I would like to serve it myself, too."

"A toast! To the happy couple," says Mr Blenkinsop.

Half an hour later Trevor is dancing wildly with the bridesmaids while the band plays 'White Wedding'.

"It's terrible!" says Philip. "Drunk and flirting with other women on his wedding day."

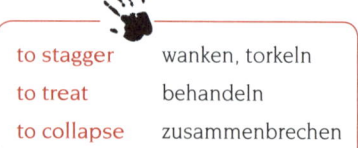

to stagger	wanken, torkeln
to treat	behandeln
to collapse	zusammenbrechen

He and Abigail watch as Trevor leaves the dance floor and **staggers** out of the room.

"How can he **treat** Sylvia so badly?" says Philip angrily. "I'm going to speak to him." He follows Trevor to the gents.

"Nice day to... start again," shouts the singer into his microphone. "It's a...nice day for a...white wedding."

"Abi, do you know where Trevor is?" Sylvia asks.

"I think he went to the gents, Sylvia. I'm sure he will..."

Suddenly the dining room door opens and Philip runs in.

"Someone help!" he shouts. "Trevor has **collapsed**. I think he's dead!"

Exercise 3: Present simple or present progressive?
Unterstreichen Sie die richtige Variante!

1. Where's Trevor? – He dances / is dancing on the dance floor.

2. Abigail works / is working for the Liverpool Constabulary.

3. She loves / is loving her job.

4. Abigail washes / is washing her hands when the door opens / is opening.

5. Stuart knows / is knowing Trevor well.

The Wedding Present

"Calm down everyone, please!" shouts Abigail. "I'm a police officer. Everyone sit down and stay where you are. Can someone help Sylvia? Quickly please!"

Mrs Blenkinsop puts her arms round Sylvia, who is crying hysterically.

"Now Philip, take me to Trevor."

Philip leads Abigail to the gents and opens the door. Trevor is lying on the floor. Abigail kneels beside him.

"I can't feel any pulse," she says. "Quick! Call an ambu-

to calm down	sich beruhigen
police officer	Polizeibeamtin
to kneel	knien
ambulance	Krankenwagen
to examine	untersuchen
heart failure	Herzversagen
overdose	Überdosis
forensic team	Spezialisten für Spurensicherung

lance. And I will call the local police station for help."

"Good evening, I'm Dr White. I came as quickly as I could," says the doctor ten minutes later. He examines Trevor. "I'm afraid he's dead – heart failure, I think."

"Doctor, I think he was taking drugs. Was it an overdose?" asks Abigail.

"It's possible," replies the doctor. "I'm sure the police forensic team will examine him carefully to find that out."

"I saw him put a packet in his pocket," says Abigail. "Let's see if it's still there."

She opens Trevor's jacket and searches the inside pocket. "It's empty!"

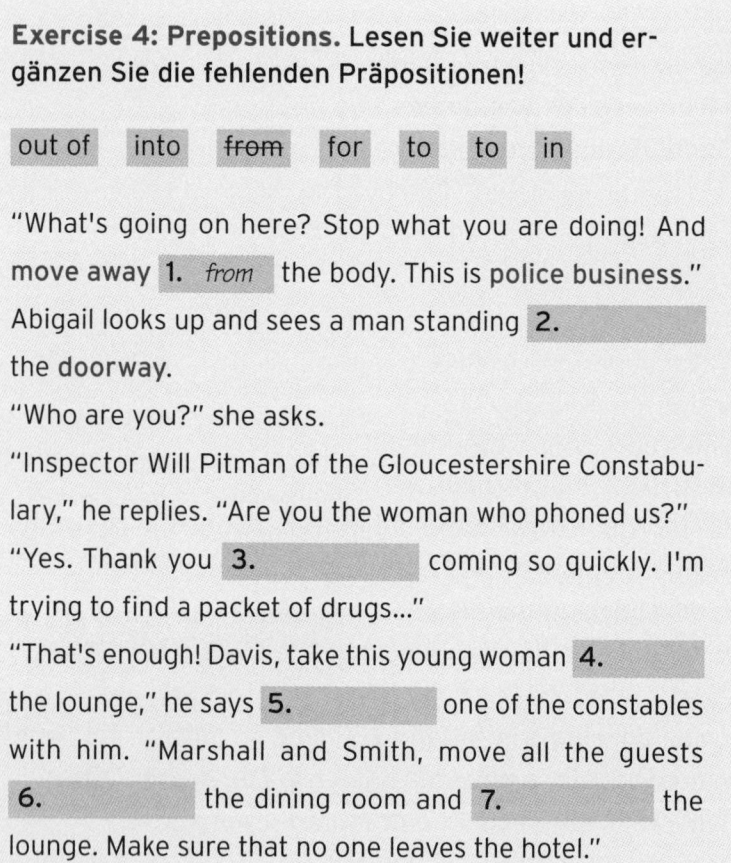

Exercise 4: Prepositions. Lesen Sie weiter und ergänzen Sie die fehlenden Präpositionen!

out of | into | ~~from~~ | for | to | to | in

"What's going on here? Stop what you are doing! And move away **1.** *from* the body. This is **police business.**"

Abigail looks up and sees a man standing **2.** the doorway.

"Who are you?" she asks.

"Inspector Will Pitman of the Gloucestershire Constabulary," he replies. "Are you the woman who phoned us?"

"Yes. Thank you **3.** coming so quickly. I'm trying to find a packet of drugs..."

"That's enough! Davis, take this young woman **4.** the lounge," he says **5.** one of the constables with him. "Marshall and Smith, move all the guests **6.** the dining room and **7.** the lounge. Make sure that no one leaves the hotel."

"Wait a moment!" Abigail holds out her police ID. "Detective Inspector Abigail Baxter," reads Pitman.

"Davis, call Liverpool and check this out. Please go and wait with the other guests, Miss Baxter."

"OK, OK, I'm going," says Abigail. "Dr White, could you come with me please? I think the bride needs a sedative."

"Smith, bring me the person who found the body.ⓘ I'll be in the conference room," says Pitman.

to search	durchsuchen
to move away	sich wegbewegen
police business	Angelegenheit der Polizei
doorway	Türöffnung
ID	Ausweis
sedative	Beruhigungs-mittel
to take a seat	Platz nehmen
angry	wütend
to deserve	verdienen

Philip enters the conference room and nervously takes a seat at the long table.

"Name, please!" says Pitman.

"Morrison, Philip Morrison."

"Mr Morrison, please tell me what happened in the gents."

"Well, I followed Trevor there. But when I opened the door, he was lying on the floor."

"Why did you follow him?" asks Pitman.

Das Wort **body** kann sowohl Körper als auch Leiche bedeuten.

"I was angry with him and I wanted to talk to him. But I was too late," says Philip.

"Why were you angry?"

"Trevor was a pig! He treated Sylvia so badly. She deserves someone better than him."

Very interesting, thinks Pitman. "Was there anyone else in the gents at the time, Mr Morrison?"

irritated	genervt, gereizt
trace	Spur
file	Datei
bald	kahlköpfig

"No, just me and Trevor."

"Excuse me, sir," says Constable Davis. "I phoned Liverpool. Inspector Baxter is not here as a police officer. She's just a wedding guest."

"OK, Davis, bring her in next," says Pitman.

"So you think Stuart Shields sold Trevor some drugs?" Pitman asks Abigail a few minutes later.

"Yes, but when I checked Trevor's body, his pockets were empty. You should search Stuart Shields quickly."

"I know how to do my job!" says Pitman, irritated.[i]

"Marshall, ask the forensic team to examine Shields for traces of drugs. And check his name in our police files. Now, Inspector Baxter, tell me everything you know."

Abigail is still talking when Constable Marshall comes in.

"Sir, the forensic doctor wants to speak to you," he says.

A small, bald man wearing little round glasses enters.

"Hello Dr Witherspoon," says Pitman. "Did you find anything interesting?"

"Yes, I did. The young lady was right," the doctor says, smiling at Abigail. "Shields has traces of cocaine inside his nose and on his clothing."

"Did you find a plastic packet?" asks Abigail.

"No, nothing, I'm afraid."

Achtung, falsche Freunde!	
irritated	gereizt
≠ irritiert	**confused**
chef	Koch/Köchin
≠ Chef(in)	**boss**

"Marshall, tell the boys to search the dining room carefully," orders Pitman. "And bring Shields to me."

"Inspector Baxter, you can go back to the lounge now. I'll manage this."

carefully	sorgfältig
criminal record	Vorstrafe
excitedly	aufgeregt
powder	Puder

Exercise 5: Match up the descriptions. Ordnen Sie die Beschreibungen richtig zu!

1. ☐ Philip Morrison a) ...is irritated by Abigail.
2. ☐ Trevor's b) ...to take a seat.
3. ☐ Will Pitman c) ...is bald.
4. ☐ Pitman tells Philip d) ...is angry with Trevor.
5. ☐ Dr Witherspoon e) ...pockets are empty.

"Mr Shields, we found traces of drugs on your clothes. And we also know from our files that you have a criminal record for drug dealing. So where are the drugs that you sold to Mr Taylor?" asks Pitman.

"I didn't sell any cocaine to Trevor! He asked me to bring some to the party. It was a wedding present – for my friend. And now he's dead!" Stuart puts his head in his hands.

"Take him to the police station. He can spend the night in a cell," Pitman says to his men.

A few minutes later Davis says excitedly, "Sir, we have found a plastic packet of white powder! "And do you know where it was? In the bride's handbag!"

at once	sofort
⚡ to light up	eine Zigarette anzünden
Hang on!	Warte mal!
voice	Stimme
shadow	Schatten
nearly	fast
married	verheiratet

"What? Bring Sylvia Taylor here. I must talk to her at once."

"Sorry, sir. Mrs Taylor is asleep. Dr White gave her some sleeping tablets to calm her down."

"Damn! Then I'll speak to her early tomorrow morning," says Pitman. "Give the powder to Dr Witherspoon. Tell him to examine it as soon as possible."

Much later, Abigail is lying in bed, but she can't sleep.

It was such a strange day. I really need a cigarette, she thinks.

She gets out of bed, gets dressed and walks very quietly along the corridor and down the stairs. Outside, she stands next to a rose bush and lights up.

Ahh, that's better! she thinks. Hang on! What's that? I can hear voices.

In the moonlight she sees the shadows of two men on the other side of the garden. Quietly, she moves closer and listens carefully.

"I think it's better like this. Better for Sylvia without him!"

> **Question tags** (Frageanhängsel) werden verwendet, um vom Gesprächspartner eine Bestätigung oder Zustimmung zu erhalten. Auf Deutsch würde man fragen „oder?", „nicht wahr?"
> *You live here, **don't you?***
> *You don't like Trevor, **do you?***

"Yes, sir. I agree. You know he only wanted her money, don't you?" ⓘ

"Yes, Philip. I heard about his love affair. It nearly broke my heart to see my lovely daughter married to a man like that!"

"But now she's free again, isn't she?" says Philip, and both men laugh quietly.

Well that's two people who are happy to see Trevor dead! thinks Abigail.

Exercise 6: Questions tags. Vervollständigen Sie die folgenden Fragen mit Frageanhängseln!

1. You are Trevor's friend,   ?

2. Stuart lives in London,   ?

3. Sylvia is single again,   ?

4. You work in Liverpool,   ?

5. Philip doesn't like Trevor,   ?

A Deadly Cocktail

Early the next morning, Inspector Pitman's phone rings and wakes him up.

plant	Pflanze
poisonous	giftig

"It's Witherspoon here. I've got some interesting news."

"My God, man! It's six o'clock in the morning[1]!"

"Yes, I worked all night and examined Taylor. Now listen to this. I found traces of cocaine, just like on Stuart Shields. But I also found something else – a high dose of digitalis."

"Digitalis? What's that?" asks Pitman.

"It's a very interesting organic substance. You can find it in some plants. Doctors sometimes use it to treat patients with weak hearts."

"So are you saying that Trevor Taylor had a weak heart? Is that why he died?" asks Pitman.

"No. Taylor was a strong young man. He definitely did not need medicine for his heart. But there was a lot of digitalis in Trevor's blood. And in high doses it is very poisonous."

> Im Englischen verwendet man bei der Uhrzeit meistens das 12-Stunden-System. Um Verwechslungen vorzubeugen, ergänzt man für Vormittag **a.m.** (ante meridiem, *Latein*) und für Nachmittag **p.m.** (post meridiem, *Latein*). Oder man verwendet die Angaben **in the morning / in the afternoon / in the evening / at night.**
> z.B. *8 p.m. = 8 o'clock in the evening.*

"So it was poison! Good work, Witherspoon."

"Yes, and there's something else," says Witherspoon. "Do you remember the white powder in Sylvia Taylor's handbag? I tested it. It's a mixture of cocaine and digitalis."

Exercise 7: Opposites. Wie lautet das Gegenteil der folgenden Begriffe?

1. strong   _____
2. low   _____
3. boring   _____
4. late   _____
5. old   _____

"Wake up, Shields!" says Pitman twenty minutes later at the police station. "Did you sell poisoned drugs to the Taylors?"

"I don't know what you mean!" shouts Shields.

"Someone poisoned Trevor Taylor. And I think you know something about it!"

"Why me? There was nothing wrong with my coke. Trevor and I took some together early in the afternoon. It was good stuff! And I had no reason to hurt Trevor. He was my friend. Why don't you ask that cow he married? She had a motive."

"What do you mean?" asks Pitman.

mixture	Mischung
⚡ coke	Koks
⚡ stuff	Zeug
to hurt sb.	jmd. verletzen

complicated	kompliziert
to nod	nicken
butterfly	Schmetterling
rude	gemein

"Well, let's say Trevor's personal life was complicated."
"Do you mean he was having an affair?"

Shields nods. "There was another woman. Trevor met her in a nightclub in London."

"What's her name?" asks Pitman.

"He called her 'M'. I don't know her full name."

"Did he tell you anything else about her?"

"Oh yes. He said she was very pretty. And she's got a tattoo behind her ear – a little butterfly."

A butterfly! thinks Pitman. That won't help me to find her.

"One more question," says Pitman. "Why are you so rude about Sylvia? Do you have a problem with her?"

"Sylvia? I'll tell you why. Trevor and I were old friends. But she told Trevor not to invite me to the wedding. Of course, he didn't listen. As I said, he and I were good friends."

Exercise 8: True or false? Welche Aussagen sind korrekt? Markieren Sie mit richtig ✔ oder falsch – !

1. Trevor died because he took too much cocaine. ❒

2. Digitalis is a medicine. ❒

3. Stuart doesn't know Trevor's girlfriend. ❒

4. Stuart and Sylvia are good friends. ❒

At 8 a.m. in the Manor House Hotel, someone knocks loudly on Abigail's bedroom door.

"Who's there?" she shouts.

"It's Will Pitman. I need to talk to you. Can I come in?"

"One moment!" she replies.

She gets dressed quickly and opens the door.

"Good morning, Inspector," says Pitman.

He walks into the room and closes the door behind him. "I've got some interesting news."

He tells Abigail about his phone call with Dr Witherspoon and his talk with Stuart Shields.

surprised	überrascht
to murder	ermorden
to contain	ent-/beinhalten
to question sb.	jmd. befragen
to hurry	sich beeilen
nightmare	Albtraum

"Poison!" says Abigail surprised. "Do you think someone murdered Trevor?"

"It looks that way," says Pitman. "My men found a plastic packet in your friend's handbag. Witherspoon says it contains cocaine mixed with a lot of digitalis – more than enough to kill a man."

"Sylvia?" Abigail is shocked by the news.

"That's why I'm here. I'm trying to question Mrs Taylor, but she won't stop crying. Could you come and help?"

"Of course!" says Abigail.

She and Pitman hurry to the conference room.

"Oh, Abigail! It's a nightmare!" cries Sylvia when she sees her friend. "They say someone murdered Trevor. And they think it was me! It's crazy! I loved him. Please tell them!"

Abigail sits down next to Sylvia and holds her hand.

"I'm sure it wasn't you, Sylvia. But you have to help the police [i] with their investigation. Tell us about the packet in your handbag."

"I don't know anything about a packet. I didn't put it there!" Sylvia starts to cry loudly.

Exercise 9: Past simple. Lesen Sie weiter und setzen Sie die Verben in der einfachen Vergangenheitsform ein!

"I know this is very hard for you, but I have to ask you something," says Abigail. " **1.** know _____Did you know_____ that Trevor **2.** have _____ a lover?"

"That's not true! I know there **3.** be _____ someone. But it **4.** finish _____ **a long time ago**. He **5.** tell _____ her he **6.** not want _____ her. He only loved me!"

"And you believed him?"
"Yes, of course!" Sylvia cries. The door opens and Constable Marshall comes in.
"What is it, Marshall? Can't you see we're busy!" says Pitman impatiently.
"Sorry, sir, but Dr Witherspoon called. He wants you and Inspector Baxter to come to his lab. He says it's important."

> Einige Sammelbegriffe verlangen ein Plural-Verb, wenn man darunter eine Gruppe von Menschen versteht, u. a.
> **police, press, public** und **team**:
> z.B. _The police **are** trying to find the murderer._
> _My team **are** playing well today._

A quarter of an hour later, Abigail and Pitman arrive at Dr Witherspoon's forensic lab. The air **smells** strongly **of** chemicals. There is a body lying on the table under a green plastic sheet. Abigail **shivers**.

"Come closer. I want to show you something interesting," says Dr Witherspoon.

He lifts the plastic sheet to show Trevor's face. Trevor's face is very **pale** and there are dark shadows around his eyes.

"Look. This is where I found traces of cocaine," says Dr

investigation	Ermittlung
a long time ago	vor langer Zeit
to believe	glauben
busy	beschäftigt
impatiently	ungeduldig
lab (*Abk.* laboratory)	Labor
to smell of	nach etw. riechen
to shiver	erschauern
pale	blass
pure	rein
tongue	Zunge
throat	Rachen
stomach	Magen

Witherspoon. "Around his nose and inside it, too. And here's the interesting point. The cocaine I found there was **pure**. There are no traces of other medicines or drugs[1] there. But the digitalis," he says, opening Trevor's mouth, "was here on his **tongue**. And also in his **throat** and **stomach**."

"What does that mean?" asks Pitman.

"That the poison was not mixed with the cocaine!" Abigail replies.

"Right!" says Witherspoon.

> Das Wort **drug** bedeutet nicht nur Droge, sondern auch Medikament oder Arzneimittel.

"It was probably in something that he ate."

It's lunch time now and Abigail and Pitman are sitting in a café near the forensic lab.

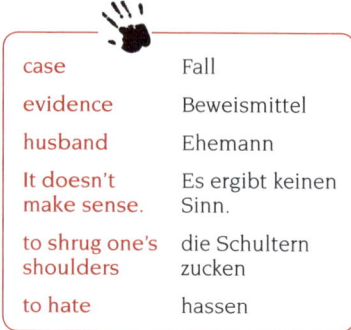

case	Fall
evidence	Beweismittel
husband	Ehemann
It doesn't make sense.	Es ergibt keinen Sinn.
to shrug one's shoulders	die Schultern zucken
to hate	hassen

"This case is very complicated," says Abigail.

"No, I think it's simple," replies Pitman. "I know she's your friend, but you can't ignore the evidence. It's like this: Sylvia knows about her husband's affair. She wants to poison him. During the meal she puts some digitalis in Trevor's food."

"No, that doesn't make sense," says Abigail. "Why does she marry him if she wants to kill him? And another thing: the powder in her handbag is a mix of cocaine and poison. Who gave her the cocaine? Stuart Shields? But the cocaine that he and Trevor took was pure. How do you explain that?"

Pitman shrugs his shoulders.

"So you see, it's not simple at all," says Abigail. "And what about Philip Morrison? He hated Trevor. And so did Sylvia's father. I think we should question Philip again. And Mr Blenkinsop."

4 A Family Affair

Back at the hotel lounge, the wedding guests are getting impatient.

"How long must we stay here?" asks a man in a business suit. "I have to get back to work!"

"Please, everyone, calm down!"

ridiculous	lächerlich
frightened	verängstigt
anxiously	besorgt, nervös

says Constable Smith. "We are working as fast as we can!"

"Why are they searching my kitchen? It's ridiculous!" says Mr Craddock, the chef. He is sitting at a table with a waiter and a group of waitresses who look frightened and unhappy. "My kitchen is one of the best in England. I am a Michelin star chef. Do they really think I poison the guests?"

Exercise 10: Pronouns. Lesen Sie weiter und ergänzen Sie die fehlenden Pronomen!

she   him   her   our   your   you

"This way, sir," says Constable Davis to Sylvia's father.

"Please sit down, Mr Blenkinsop," says Pitman. "Inspector Baxter and I have some questions to ask **1.** ."

"Abigail?" Sylvia's father looks at **2.** anxiously.

"It's OK, Rupert," **3.**   says. "It's just part of **4.**   routine investigation."

"Mr Blenkinsop, tell us about **5.**   **relationship** with Trevor Taylor," says Pitman.

"I didn't know **6.**   very well. Sylvia didn't bring him home very often."

"Why not?" Pitman asks Mr Blenkinsop.

"Well, the truth is, I never liked Trevor. Sylvia knew that. I told her she could find someone much better. Young Philip, for example. Abigail, you know how it was at school. Philip has always loved Sylvia."

"Yes, I remember. But she wasn't interested in him. I was surprised to see him at the wedding."

"I told Sylvia to invite him," **ⓘ** says Blenkinsop. "He's our accountant now. The company is **doing very well** and Philip is a big help. He's almost part of the family."

"You say your company is doing well, Mr Blenkinsop," says Pitman.

"Yes, very well. But my wife and I will retire soon. My doctor says I should rest. I have some heart problems, you see."

> Tell und **say** bedeuten beide „sagen", werden aber unterschiedlich verwendet:
>
> **to say sth.**   etw. sagen
> **to tell sb. sth.**   jmd. etw. sagen
> **to tell sb. to**   jmd. sagen, dass
>   **do sth.**   er etw. tun soll
> z.B.
> *Tell* me what happened.
> *Pitman **tells** Abigail to wait in the lounge.*
> *She **says** that she is a police officer.*

"I'm sorry to hear that, Rupert," says Abigail.

"Oh, it's nothing serious, my dear. And I've got some good medication. So I don't feel too bad."

"Heart medication?" asks Pitman. "Tell us exactly what you are taking."

Blenkinsop looks confused. "Why do you need to know that? I thought this was about Trevor."

"Just answer the question!" says Pitman impatiently.

"Rupert, please?" says Abigail and gives him a kindly smile.

"Just beta blockers," Blenkinsop replies.

"Do you know what digitalis is?" asks Pitman.

"Digitalis? Well, yes. Last year my doctor gave me some medicine called

relationship	Beziehung
to do well	Erfolg haben
serious	ernst
confused	verwirrt
kindly	sanft, freundlich
side effect	Nebenwirkung
cabinet	Schrank
to train	*hier*: einarbeiten

Digiton... or Digitan, something like that. I think it contained digitalis. But I didn't take it for long. The side effects, you know."

"Have you still got the medicine?" asks Abigail.

"Yes, it's still in the bathroom cabinet. I don't like to throw things away."

"Another question," says Pitman. "What happens to your company when you and your wife retire?"

"We're training Sylvia to take over. She's doing well. I'm sure she can manage the company alone."

"Alone? Yes, of course, now that her husband is dead!"

says Pitman. "You didn't want Trevor running the company with her, did you?"

Blenkinsop doesn't answer.

"You say you've got a **dangerous** drug in your bathroom cabinet. You were sitting near Trevor at dinner. You could easily put something in his food," says Pitman.

to run the company	die Firma leiten
dangerous	gefährlich
proof	Beweis
search warrant	Durchsuchungs-befehl

"That's absurd! And you've got no **proof**!" shouts Sylvia's father angrily.

"Davis," says Pitman, "get me a **search warrant** for the Blenkinsops' house."

Exercise 11: Tell or say? Unterstreichen Sie die richtige Variante!

1. Say / Tell us what medicine you are talking.

2. Philip says / tells Abigail that he is an accountant.

3. The doctor says / tells that Trevor is dead.

4. Say / Tell me what to do!

5. "Just answer the question!" says / tells Pitman.

"What do you think?" Pitman asks Abigail after Mr Blenkinsop leaves the room. "You know the family well."

"Yes, I do. Rupert Blenkinsop is a very kind man... normally. Inspector, I must tell you something." Abigail tells Pitman what she heard at night in the rose garden.

| to stare at sth. | etw. anstarren |
| to notice | merken |

"But I just can't imagine that Rupert is a killer," she says.

"Remember that he's a father who wants the best for his daughter and for his company," says Pitman. "And he had the poison in his house."

"Perhaps you're right. But Philip also has a strong motive. Let's talk to him again while we're waiting for the search warrant."

"Mr Morrison, you told us yesterday that you were angry with Trevor Taylor. You also said that Sylvia deserves someone better. Did you mean yourself[i]?" Pitman asks.

"Why not? Sylvia and I have known each other since we were children. She's a very special person. She deserves someone who treats her well."

"So how did you feel when you heard she wanted to marry Trevor?" asks Abigail.

Philip stares at the floor and doesn't speak. Abigail notices that his hands are shaking.

Reflexivpronomen
Reflexivpronomen wie **yourself** werden verwendet, wenn sich das Pronomen auf das Subjekt des Satzes bezieht.
*He introduced **himself**.*
Er stellte **sich** vor.

"Philip?" she asks. "Is it really so difficult for you to talk about it?"

"Excuse me," interrupts Constable Marshall. "The forensic team have found something in the dining room. I think you should come at once."

| to point | hinzeigen, weisen auf |

"OK, we're coming. Morrison, I'll speak to you again later," says Pitman.

He and Abigail hurry to the dining room.

Exercise 12: Correct the mistakes. Lesen Sie weiter und korrigieren Sie die sechs Fehler!

"We found some digitalis in this champagne glass," says a forensic officer and points too a glass on the main tabel. "This is where Taylor was sitting. So someone put poison in his glass," says Pitman.

"Well, no, that's the strange think. Look at the glass. Its got lipstick on it. I don't think this was Mr Taylor's glass."

"He's write," says Abigail. "Pale pink lipstick. The same colour as Sylvia's. Were is she now?"

"In the lounge with the others," says Constable Marshall.

"We need to talk to her at once," says Abigail.

1. _____   2. _____

3. _____   4. _____

5. _____   6. _____

5 Plan B

Pitman and Abigail find Sylvia sitting on a sofa next to her mother. Mrs Blenkinsop has her arms round her daughter. Sylvia is crying.

"Sylvia, Inspector Pitman and I need to talk to you. Please come with us," says Abigail.

tears *pl*	Tränen
place mat	Platzdeckchen

"No, Abi! Please let me stay here with mum!" Tears roll down Sylvia's face.

"My poor daughter is still in shock! Can't you question her here?" asks Mrs Blenkinsop.

"OK, if you want. Sylvia, we found some poison in a champagne glass. The glass was on Trevor's place mat. But it has pink lipstick on it. Was it yours [i]?"

"I didn't drink much champagne, only a little bit at the start of the dinner," Sylvia replies. "After that I gave my glass to Trevor."

> Das Possessivpronomen **your** wird als Adjektiv verwendet, z.B. *Is it **your** glass?*
> Hingegen wird **yours**, wie hier im Satz, als Substantiv verwendet: *Is this glass **yours**.*

"So you gave him the poison!" says Pitman.

"I didn't know the champagne was poisoned!" Sylvia cries.

"Then why didn't you drink it?" asks Pitman.

"Because I'm pregnant!"

Exercise 13: Verb forms. Lesen Sie weiter und setzen Sie die Verben in der richtigen Form ein!

"What?" says Mrs Blenkinsop in surprise. "Darling, why

1. not tell _____ you _____ us?"

"I **2. want** _____ to tell Trevor first – on our wedding night." Sylvia starts to cry again.

"I **3. not understand** _____," says Pitman.

"Does this mean that Taylor **4. die** _____ by mistake?

So the killer really wanted **5. kill** _____..."

"Oh my God!" says Sylvia. She turns very white and

6. fall _____ back against the sofa.

"Quickly, Sarah and Emma, fetch some water and a blanket for the lady!" shouts Mr Craddock.

Two waitresses, one blonde, one dark-haired, jump up.

"Come on, Em, I'll get the blanket. You fetch the water," says the blonde one.

Em? thinks Abigail. Of course!

"Wait a minute, girls. Tell me your full names."

by mistake	aus Versehen
fetch	herbeiholen
blanket	Decke

"I'm Sarah Smith," says the blonde waitress.

The other girl just stands and stares at the floor.

"And this is Emma Jenkins," says Mr Craddock.

"Miss Jenkins, do people call you Em?" asks Abigail.

"Close friends call me Em," whispers the dark-haired girl.

"Could you come closer, please," says Abigail. "And pull back your hair."

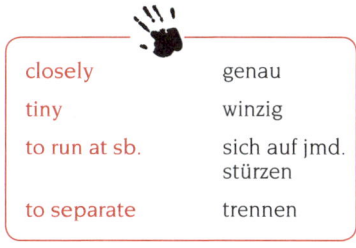

closely	genau
tiny	winzig
to run at sb.	sich auf jmd. stürzen
to separate	trennen

Emma's hands are shaking as she pulls her thick black hair away from her ears.

Abigail looks closely. Behind Emma's left ear she sees a tattoo – a tiny butterfly.

"So you are the mysterious M! Trevor's lover. Of course, Em, not M!" says Abigail.

"What?" screams Sylvia, the colour returning to her cheeks.

"Yes," says Emma, crying. "Trevor didn't love you! He wanted to be with me!"

Sylvia runs at Emma and knocks her to the floor.

"Stop this at once! Emma Jenkins, I must ask you to come with us to the police station," shouts Pitman as his constables separate the two women.

The next day, Abigail meets Dr Witherspoon in the café near the forensic lab. He can't wait to hear the whole story.

"So Emma poisoned Trevor by mistake! Tell me more!" **i**

"Emma and Trevor had a plan," explains Abigail. "They wanted to kill Sylvia and then run off with Sylvia's money."

> Die Befehlsform (Imperativ) wird mit dem Infinitiv ohne **to** gebildet: *Tell* me more! Erzähl(t) mir mehr!

"On her wedding day? How dramatic!" says Witherspoon.

| after all | doch (nicht) |
| suspect | Verdächtiger |

"Yes, isn't it? And clever. First, Emma works at the Manor House Hotel. So Trevor tells Sylvia it is the perfect place for the wedding party. And of course Sylvia has no idea that Trevor's lover is a waitress there. They want to poison Sylvia, but the police should think it was someone else. So Trevor invites Stuart Shields to the party. And he asks Shields to bring some cocaine with him."

Exercise 14: Definitions. Ordnen Sie den Wörtern die passende Definition zu!

1. ☐ to get sth. and bring it back   **a)** to shout
2. ☐ very, very small   **b)** to whisper
3. ☐ to speak very loudly   **c)** to stare
4. ☐ to speak very quietly   **d)** tiny
5. ☐ to look very hard at sth.   **e)** butterfly
6. ☐ a beautiful insect that loves flowers   **f)** to fetch

"But Shields is his friend, isn't he?" asks Witherspoon.
"It seems they are not such good friends after all," explains Abigail. "And Shields and Sylvia hate each other. So Shields is the perfect suspect for Sylvia's murder. Shields gives Trevor a packet of cocaine as a wedding present. Trevor takes the packet to the kitchen and gives it to Emma."
"But he takes some cocaine first," says Witherspoon.

"Yes, he's **greedy**. And he wants to enjoy the party before things get serious," says Abigail.

greedy	gierig
to decide	entscheiden
proud	stolz

"So what happens next?" asks Dr Witherspoon.

"Well, Emma mixes the poison with the cocaine. While Sylvia is busy talking to her guests, Emma puts the packet in her handbag. She wants the police to find it there after Sylvia's death. She wants us to think that Shields gave Sylvia poisoned drugs."

"Very clever! But what about the poisoned champagne? Why does Trevor drink it? Doesn't he know it's poisoned?"

"This is where the plan goes wrong. Emma wants to put the digitalis in Sylvia's piece of wedding cake. But at the last minute, Mr Craddock **decides** to serve the cake himself. He is so **proud** of his creation."

"Yes, isn't he? I don't know how many times he told me about his Michelin star," says Witherspoon with a laugh. "So does Emma have a Plan B?"

"Not really. She has to improvise. Mr Craddock tells her to serve the champagne. So she puts the poison in Sylvia's glass. She has no idea that Sylvia is pregnant. Then Sylvia gives her glass to Trevor, and you know the rest."

"What an interesting story. But where did Trevor and Emma get the digitalis from? Mr Blenkinsop's medicine cabinet?"

"That's right. We searched his house and the bottle of tablets was not there. Rupert remembers seeing it in the cabinet a month ago. Here's his story: Sylvia and Trevor come

Cheer up!	Kopf hoch!
to solve	lösen
to celebrate	feiern

to dinner one evening. Rupert has a headache. So he goes to the bathroom to get some aspirin. When he opens the cabinet, he sees the bottle of digitalis. He remembers thinking that he should take it back to the chemist's.  That was the last time he remembers seeing the bottle."

"So Trevor took it?"

"So it seems. But we can't ask him, can we? Poor Sylvia! How terrible for her," says Abigail sadly.

Die gebräuchlichere Kurzform von **the chemist's shop** (Apotheke) ist **the chemist's.** Andere Beispiele sind:
the baker's   Bäckerei
the butcher's   Metzgerei

"Cheer up, Abigail. You solved the crime. Let's celebrate! How about some champagne?" asks Witherspoon, smiling. "No, thank you!" says Abigail. "But I'd like a nice cup of tea!"

And they both laugh.

Final Test

Exercise 1: Translation match-up. Wie lautet die richtige Übersetzung? Ordnen Sie zu!

1. ☐ terrible   **a)** gierig

2. ☐ poisonous   **b)** eifersüchtig

3. ☐ jealous   **c)** Turnhalle

4. ☐ greedy   **d)** Chef

5. ☐ frightened   **e)** giftig

6. ☐ mobile phone   **f)** furchtbar

7. ☐ boss   **g)** verängstigt

8. ☐ gym   **h)** Handy

Exercise 2: Verb forms. Wie lautet das Present Simple und Past Simple der folgenden Verben in der dritten Person?

1. to find   *finds*   *found*

2. to see   _____   _____

3. to sell   _____   _____

4. to give   _____   _____

5. to take   _____   _____

Exercise 3: Word spiral! Füllen Sie die Wortspirale und finden Sie den Beruf der Mörderin!

1 K	2 N	3 O	4 W	5	6
20	21	22	23	24	7
19	32	33	34	25	8
18	31	36	35	26	9
17	30	29	28	27	10
16	15	14	13	12	11

1-4:   Do you ... the answer?
4-10:   to speak very quietly
10-15: to come back
15-19: opposite of always
19-26: opposite of forget
26-33: The man is ... the newspaper.
32-36: The poison is in the ....

Lösung: __ __ __ __ __ __ __ __

Exercise 4: True or false? Welche Aussagen sind korrekt? Kreuzen Sie an!

1. Anne Sophie sees Old George running from the yacht. ❒
2. A fisherman finds the capsized boat. ❒
3. Roger Hartley's ex-wife planned the murder. ❒
4. Abigail was at school with Sylvia and Philip. ❒
5. Trevor wanted to kill his wife. ❒
6. Emma wanted to kill Trevor. ❒

Exercise 5: Spot the mistake. Welcher Satz ist fehlerfrei? Kreuzen Sie an!

1. a) ❑ Old George is working when Hartley arrives.
   b) ❑ Old George works when Hartley arrives.

2. a) ❑ I am thinking you should call the police!
   b) ❑ I think you should call the police!

3. a) ❑ Bad news travels fast.
   b) ❑ Bad news travel fast.

4. a) ❑ Say me the whole story.
   b) ❑ Tell me the whole story.

5. a) ❑ The police is looking for the murderer.
   b) ❑ The police are looking for the murderer.

6. a) ❑ Is this Trevors' glass? No, it's Sylvias'.
   b) ❑ Is this Trevor's glass? No, it's Sylvia's.

Exercise 6: Pronouns. Ersetzen Sie die markierten Wörter durch die entsprechenden Pronomen!

1. James taps her fingers while waiting for **Ross**. ___*him*___

2. **Megan's parents** died a few years ago. _____

3. Interview all of **the teachers**. _____

4. He asks **Anna** many questions. _____

5. He puts **three notes** on the table. _____

6. **Jonathan** doesn't eat much dinner. _____

7. **Anna and I** are eating pasta. _____

8. Rupert sees **the bottle of digitalis**. _____

Exercise 7: Vocabulary pairs. Welche Begriffe gehören zusammen? Ordnen Sie zu!

1. ☐ to keep   **a)** sense
2. ☐ to tell   **b)** a seat
3. ☐ to get   **c)** down
4. ☐ to calm   **d)** a secret
5. ☐ to take   **e)** rid of
6. ☐ to make   **f)** the truth

Exercise 8: Plurals. Bilden Sie die richtige Pluralformen!

1. student   *students*
2. man   _____
3. class   _____
4. homework   _____

Exercise 9: Idioms. Übersetzen Sie folgende Sätze ins Englische!

1. Ihre Worte kamen aus heiterem Himmel.

   _____

2. Sie ist sehr klug. Es liegt in der Familie.

   _____

3. Er hat ihr das Herz gebrochen.

   _____

4. Ich habe Schmetterlinge im Bauch!

   _____

 **Answers**

Death at Land's End

Exercise 1: 1. large 2. noisy 3. unfriendly 4. expensive

Exercise 2: 1. true 2. true 3. false (He calls the coast-guard.) 4. false (McGregor works with his partner, Sam Nolan.) 5. false (He smokes a cigarette and watches the sun set.)

Exercise 3: 1. repeats 2. tells 3. tell 4. is 5. get

Exercise 4: 1. you're (your) 2. tell (say) 3. it (him) 4. easily (easy) 5. thinks (things) 6. German (german)

Exercise 5: 1. d 2. c 3. b 4. a

Exercise 6: 1. O'Reilly doesn't think she is a liar.
2. Did you see him?
3. They identify his body.
4. Walker keeps it at Sennen Cove.
5. Do you believe her?

Exercise 7: 1. onto 2. to 3. to 4. for 5. on 6. at

Exercise 8: 1. nosy 2. nasty 3. dirty 4. empty 5. angry

Exercise 9: 1. When 2. What 3. Where 4. who

Exercise 10: 1. sit down 2. husband 3. lost 4. love 5. strong

Exercise 11: 1. name's 2. I'm 3. She's 4. isn't 5. We'll

Exercise 12: 1. false (Walker went to Cornwall to sail his yacht one last time.) 2. true 3. true 4. false (Giles often goes sailing. He lied to O'Reilly.)

Exercise 13: 1. Where 2. What is 3. her 4. men 5. thinks

Exercise 14: 1. are you going 2. be 3. Are 4. has 5. goes

Exercise 15:

M	A	L	W	E	M	W	O	T	S
O	V	E	R	B	O	A	R	D	A
G	K	I	S	R	T	V	D	E	I
D	E	S	U	A	O	E	A	C	B
P	E	W	R	T	R	I	C	K	O
I	L	I	F	E	B	U	O	Y	T
L	E	M	I	N	O	T	U	Z	N
L	Y	T	S	E	A	S	I	C	K
O	R	E	T	S	T	M	A	B	E
D	E	A	K	Y	A	C	H	T	E

Murder in the Classroom

Exercise 1: 1. ambulance 2. pace 3. secretary 4. ugly

Exercise 2: 1. stays 2. is making 3. finish 4. go
5. is meeting

Exercise 3: 1. c 2. d 3. e 4. b 5. a 6. f

Exercise 4: 1. false (No, it's badminton.) 2. true 3. false
(He flirts with her.) 4. true 5. false (She puts
them in her desk drawer.)

Exercise 5: 1. to 2. watching 3. write 4. says 5. at

Exercise 6: 1. to lose 2. to stand up 3. to leave 4. to forget
5. to cry

Exercise 7: 1. Am I 2. die 3. investigating 4. come
5. Are you going

Exercise 8: 1. d 2. b 3. e 4. c 5. f 6. a

Exercise 9: 1. day 2. biscuits 3. attention 4. During 5. ring
6. calling 7. answer

Exercise 10: 1. c 2. d 3. b 4. a
Exercise 11: 1. about 2. by 3. at 4. down 5. of
Exercise 12: 1. Who – Ross arrests Jonathan first. 2. What –
She can't remember anything. 3. When – She
arrives after Ross pushes the emergency
buzzer. 4. Why – She wants to kill him because
he broke her heart. 5. Where – It is lying at the
bottom of the stairs.

A Wedding to Die For

Exercise 1: 1. attractive 2. dark 3. warmly 4. politely
5. quickly
Exercise 2: 1. happy 2. happy 3. lucky 4. lucky 5. lucky
Exercise 3: 1. is dancing 2. works 3. loves 4. is washing,
opens 5. knows
Exercise 4: 1. from 2. in 3. for 4. to 5. to 6. out of 7. into
Exercise 5: 1. d 2. e 3. a 4. b 5. c
Exercise 6: 1. aren't you 2. doesn't he 3. isn't she 4. don't
you 5. does he
Exercise 7: 1. weak 2. high 3. interesting 4. early 5. young
Exercise 8: 1. false (Trevor was poisoned.) 2. true 3. true
4. false (They don't like each other.)
Exercise 9: 1. Did you know 2. had 3. was 4. finished
5. told 6. didn't want
Exercise 10: 1. you 2. her 3. she 4. our 5. your 6. him
Exercise 11: 1. Tell 2. tells 3. says 4. Tell 5. says
Exercise 12: 1. to (too) 2. table (tabel) 3. thing (think)
4. It's (Its) 5. right (write) 6. Where (Were)
Exercise 13: 1. didn't … tell 2. wanted 3. don't understand
4. died 5. to kill 6. falls
Exercise 14: 1. f 2. d 3. a 4. b 5. c 6. e

Final Test

Exercise 1: **1.** f **2.** e **3.** b **4.** a **5.** g **6.** h **7.** d **8.** c

Exercise 2: **1.** finds, found **2.** sees, saw **3.** sells, sold
4. gives, gave **5.** takes, took

Exercise 3:

1 K	2 N	3 O	4 W	5 H	6 I
20 E	21 M	22 E	23 M	24 B	7 S
19 R	32 G	33 L	34 A	25 E	8 P
18 E	31 N	36 S	35 S	26 R	9 E
17 V	30 I	29 D	28 A	27 E	10 R
16 E	15 N	14 R	13 U	12 T	11 E

Lösung: WAITRESS

Exercise 4: **1.** false (She sees Old George's son, Clive, running from the yacht.) **2.** true **3.** false (Hartley's business partner, Giles Hill, planned the murder.) **4.** true **5.** true **6.** false (She killed him by mistake.)

Exercise 5: **1.** a **2.** b **3.** a **4.** b **5.** b **6.** b

Exercise 6: **1.** him **2.** They **3.** them **4.** her **5.** them **6.** He **7.** We **8.** it

Exercise 7: **1.** d **2.** f **3.** e **4.** c **5.** b **6.** a

Exercise 8: **1.** students **2.** men **3.** classes **4.** homework

Exercise 9: **1.** Her words came out of the blue.
2. She is very clever. It runs in the family.
3. He broke her heart.
4. I have butterflies in my stomach.

 **Glossary**

$ℓ$ = umgangssprachlich
pl = Plural

accident	Unfall, Unglück
accountant	Buchhalter(in)
to act strangely	sich seltsam verhalten
a dream come true	ein wahrgewordener Traum
afloat	über Wasser
after all	doch (nicht)
against	gegen
a long time ago	vor langer Zeit
Alsace	Elsass
ambulance	Krankenwagen
angry	ärgerlich, verärgert
anxiously	besorgt, nervös
anything else	sonst noch etwas
anyway	trotzdem
to appear	erscheinen
to arrest	festnehmen
at last	endlich
at once	sofort
at the seaside	an der Küste
at top speed	mit voller Geschwindigkeit
attempted murder	versuchter Mord

attention	Aufmerksamkeit
⚡ Aye, aye!	Jawohl! Zu Befehl!
bad luck	Pech
bad news travels fast	schlechte Nachrichten verbreiten sich schnell
badge	Marke, Abzeichen
bald	kahlköpfig
bankrupt	bankrott
basically	eigentlich, im Grunde
bead	Perle
to be afraid	Angst haben
to beat (beat, beaten)	schlagen, pochen
to beg sb. for sth.	jmd. anflehen um
to believe	glauben
bell	Glocke, Klingel
to be under arrest	verhaftet sein
binoculars *pl*	Fernglas
blanket	Decke
body	*hier*: Leiche; Körper
bored	gelangweilt
bracelet	Armband
breathlessly	atemlos
bride	Braut
bridesmaid	Brautjungfer
briefcase	Aktentasche
to bump	anrempeln
business associate	Geschäftspartner(in)
business card	Visitenkarte
busy	beschäftigt
butterfly	Schmetterling
by mistake	aus Versehen
cabinet	Schrank
to calm down	sich beruhigen

can	Dose
to cancel a contract	einen Vertrag kündigen
to capsize	kentern
carefully	sorgfältig
case	Fall
cases to solve	zu lösende Fälle
to catch (caught, caught)	*hier*: einholen
to catch up	*hier*: etw. aufarbeiten
to cause	verursachen
to celebrate	feiern
cellar	Keller
to change one's mind	sich anders entschließen
charm	*hier*: Anhänger
Charming!	Wie charmant!
to check sth. out	etw. untersuchen
to cheer sb. up	jmd. aufmuntern
Cheer up!	Kopf hoch!
chef	Koch/Köchin
Chief Inspector	Hauptkommissar(in)
churchyard	Friedhof
to cling onto	sich festklammern an
closely	genau
coastguard	Küstenwache
⚡ coke	Koks
to collapse	zusammenbrechen
company	Firma, Unternehmen
complicated	kompliziert
confused	verwirrt
Constable	Wachtmeister(in)
Constabulary	Polizeibezirk
to contain	ent-/beinhalten
coroner	Gerichtsmediziner(in)
crime	Verbrechen

criminal investigation	polizeiliche Ermittlung
criminal record	Vorstrafe
to crouch	sich niederkauern
cruel	grausam
curly	lockig
curse	Fluch
to damage	beschädigen
dangerous	gefährlich
deal	Handel
to decide	entscheiden
decision	Entscheidung
deckchair	Liegestuhl
delicious	köstlich, lecker
to deserve	verdienen
desk	Schreibtisch
devastated	am Boden zerstört
dirty work	Drecksarbeit
to disappear	verschwinden
divorced	geschieden
Don't you dare!	Wag(t) es bloß nicht!
doorway	Türöffnung
to do well	Erfolg haben
to drag	schleppen
drawer	Schublade
dreadful	furchtbar, schrecklich
drinking and driving	betrunken Auto fahren
to drown	ertrinken
drunk	betrunken
drunkenly	betrunken
⚡ dump	Drecksloch
during	während
elderly	ältere(r/s)
emergency buzzer	Notfallknopf

enemy	Feind/Feindin
engine	Motor
entrance	Eingang
even	sogar
evidence	Beweis(mittel)
evidence bag	Tüte für Beweise
to examine	untersuchen
except (for)	bis auf, außer
excitedly	aufgeregt
exhausted	erschöpft
fault	Fehler
favourite	Lieblings-
female	weiblich
to fetch	herbeiholen
to fight (fought, fought) crime	das Verbrechen bekämpfen
figure	Gestalt
file	Akte, Datei
finally	endlich, schließlich
fire exit	Notausgang
flat	Wohnung
footsteps *pl*	Schritte
forensic officer	Gerichtsmediziner(in)
forensic team	Spezialisten für Spurensicherung
to forget (forgot, forgotten)	vergessen
for practice	zum Üben
freak	*hier*: außergewöhnlich
frightened	verängstigt
frightened to death	zu Tode erschreckt
frizzy	gekräuselt
to frown	die Stirn runzeln
funeral	Beerdigung
furniture	Möbel
to get hurt	verletzt werden

to get into trouble	Schwierigkeiten bekommen
to get rid of sb.	jmd. loswerden
to giggle	kichern
to give sb. a hug	jmd. umarmen
glad	froh
to go for a run	joggen gehen
to go into business	ein Geschäft gründen
good-for-nothing	Taugenichts
gorgeous	herrlich
to grab	greifen, fassen
greedy	gierig
ground floor	Erdgeschoss
⚡ gym	Turnhalle
handcuffs *pl*	Handschellen
handwriting	Handschrift
Hang on!	Warte mal!
to hang (hung, hung) up	*hier*: auflegen
harbour	Hafen
hardly	kaum
to hate	hassen
to have (had, had) a fight	streiten
headache	Kopfschmerzen
headline	Schlagzeile
headmistress	Schulleiterin
heart attack	Herzinfarkt
heart failure	Herzversagen
to hide (hid, hidden)	sich verstecken
to hit (hit, hit) sb.	jmd. schlagen
to hold (held, held) one's breath	den Atem anhalten
hood	Kapuze
to hope	hoffen
horrible	schrecklich

to hug	sich umarmen
to hurry	sich beeilen
to hurt (hurt, hurt) sb.	jmd. verletzen
husband	Ehemann
I don't care!	Ist mir egal!
ID	Ausweis
I'm afraid	Es tut mir leid, aber ...; leider
imagination	Fantasie
impatiently	ungeduldig
to impress sb.	jmd. beeindrucken
in despair	verzweifelt
in his mid-40s	Mitte vierzig
in the distance	in der Ferne
instead	stattdessen
investigation	Ermittlung
irritated	genervt, gereizt
It doesn't make sense.	Es ergibt keinen Sinn.
It runs in the family.	Es liegt in der Familie.
jealous	neidisch; eifersüchtig
journey	Reise
to jump up	aufspringen
keel	Kiel
keen	leidenschaftlich, eifrig
to keep an eye on sb.	jmd. im Auge behalten
to keep a secret	ein Geheimnis bewahren
kindly	sanft, freundlich
to kneel (knelt, knelt)	knien
lab (Abk. laboratory)	Labor
label	Etikett
ladies' cloakroom	Damentoilette
landlady/landlord	Wirtin/Wirt
to lead (led, led)	führen
to lean against sth.	lehnen an

to let (let, let) sb. down	jmd. im Stich lassen
letter of resignation	Kündingungsschreiben
liar	Lügner(in)
lifeboat	Rettungsboot
life buoy	Rettungsboje
to light (lit, lit)	*hier*: anzünden
⚡ to light up	eine Zigarette anzünden
local man	Einheimische(r)
locker room	Umkleide
to look forward to sth.	sich auf etw. freuen
to lose one's balance	das Gleichgewicht verlieren
lump	Beule
mad	verrückt
mainland England	das englische Festland
married	verheiratet
meanwhile	währenddessen
to meow	miauen
mess	Durcheinander
middle-aged	mittleren Alters
miserably	traurig, niedergeschlagen
missing persons report	Vermisstenanzeige
mixture	Mischung
to move	*hier*: umziehen
to move away	sich wegbewegen
to murder	ermorden
murder	Mord
murderer	Mörder(in)
nasty	gemein
nearly	fast
neighbour	Nachbar(in)
nightmare	Albtraum
to nod	nicken
noisy	laut

nosy	neugierig
to not be allowed to do sth.	etw. nicht tun dürfen
note	Notiz; Zettel
to notice	merken
office	Büro
on duty	im Dienst
one's stomach is in knots	einen verkrampften Magen haben
only child	Einzelkind
to order	befehlen
originally	ursprünglich
outline	Umriss
out of the blue	aus heiterem Himmel
over and over	immer wieder
overdose	Überdosis
package	Paket
pale	blass
paramedic	Sanitäter(in)
to pass	vorbeigehen
path	Pfad, Weg
PE (Physical Education)	Sportunterricht
pearl necklace	Perlenkette
pigeonhole	Postfach, Ablage
pipe	Tabakspfeife
place mat	Platzdeckchen
plant	Pflanze
to point	hinzeigen, weisen auf
poison	Gift
poisonous	giftig
police business	Angelegenheit der Polizei
police officer	Polizeibeamte(r)
potential	möglich
to pour	einschenken
powder	Puder

pregnant	schwanger
to prepare	vorbereiten
primary school	Grundschule
probably	wahrscheinlich
proof	Beweis
to protect	beschützen
proud	stolz
pupil	Schüler(in)
pure	rein
to put the phone down	auflegen
to question sb.	jmd. befragen
racket	Schläger
to reach sb.	jmd. erreichen
red herring	falsche Fährte
relationship	Beziehung
to remember	sich erinnern (an)
report	Bericht
rescue officer	Rettungshelfer(in)
restless	unruhig
to retire	in Rente gehen
ridiculous	lächerlich
right away	sofort
to ring (rang, rung)	läuten; anrufen
rubbery	gummiartig
rubbish	Müll
rude	gemein
rumour	Gerücht
to run (ran, run) at sb.	sich auf jmd. stürzen
to run (ran, run) past	vorbeirennen
to run the company	die Firma leiten
to rush	hasten, sausen
safety	Sicherheit
sailor	Matrose

scared	verängstigt
school grounds *pl*	Schulgelände
to scream	schreien
to search	durchsuchen
search warrant	Durchsuchungsbefehl
seasick	seekrank
sedative	Beruhigungsmittel
selfish	egoistisch
to separate	trennen
serious	ernst
seriously	ernsthaft, wirklich
to serve	servieren
to set	*hier*: untergehen
several times	mehrmals
shadow	Schatten
to shake (shook, shaken)	zittern
She didn't want me to know.	Sie wollte nicht, dass ich es erfahre.
shelf	Regal
shiny	glänzend
to shiver	erschauern, zittern
to shrug one's shoulders	die Schultern zucken
side effect	Nebenwirkung
slim	schlank
smell	Geruch
to smell of	nach etw. riechen
to sneak	schleichen
sober	nüchtern
to solve	lösen
son-in-law	Schwiegersohn
to spit (spat, spat)	spucken
to splash	schwappen
to stab	(zu)stechen

to stagger	wanken, torkeln
to stare at sth.	etw. anstarren
statement	Aussage
steering wheel	Lenkrad
still	*hier*: trotzdem; noch
stomach	Magen
strange	*hier*: merkwürdig, seltsam
strict	streng
⚡ stuff	Zeug
suddenly	plötzlich
suit	Anzug
supplier	Lieferant
surprised	überrascht
suspect	Verdächtige(r)
suspicious	verdächtig
sweet	süß
sweets *pl*	Süßigkeiten
sweet wrapper	Bonbonpapier
to take (took, taken) a deep breath	tief einatmen
to take (took, taken) a seat	Platz nehmen
tape	Klebeband
to taste	schmecken
tears *pl*	Tränen
terraced house	Reihenhaus
terrible	furchtbar, schrecklich
⚡ the gents	Herrentoilette
The Jolly Roger	Totenkopfflagge, *wörtl.*: der fröhliche Roger
the washing up	der Abwasch
throat	Rachen
tied	gefesselt
to tighten	sich zusammenziehen, enger werden

tiny	winzig
to tiptoe	auf Zehenspitzen schleichen
tissue	Papiertaschentuch
tongue	Zunge
torch	Taschenlampe
To the happy couple!	Auf das Brautpaar!
trace	Spur
to train	*hier*: einarbeiten
trap door	Falltür
trapped	gefangen
to treat	behandeln
to tremble	zittern
trolley	Servierwagen
truth	Wahrheit
unconscious	bewusstlos
unemployed	arbeitslos
to untie	losbinden
vicar	Gemeindepfarrer
voice	Stimme
wave	Welle
wedding	Hochzeit
Welsh	walisisch
to whisper	flüstern
wife	Ehefrau
to wink	zwinkern
witness	Zeuge/Zeugin
to wonder	sich fragen
worried	besorgt
to worry about	sich Sorgen machen um
wrist	Handgelenk
yet	schon, bis jetzt

List of Exercises

Compact Lernkrimis auch in Spanisch, Französisch, Italienisch, Deutsch und Schwedisch erhältlich.

Compact Lernkrimi
Classic

A1		

A2		

B1

Art and Ashes
ISBN 978-3-8174-9493-4

Cook and Kill
ISBN 978-3-8174-9492-7

Crime Scene Tower of London
ISBN 978-3-8174-7687-9

Deadly Mistake
ISBN 978-3-8174-8259-7

Death Wasn't the Deal
ISBN 978-3-8174-9491-0

Der Rächer von Canterbury
ISBN 978-3-8174-7662-6

Der rote Nebel
ISBN 978-3-8174-7574-2

Ein fast perfekter Coup
ISBN 978-3-8174-7568-1

Game Over in Soho
ISBN 978-3-8174-7878-1

Hunting the Vampire
ISBN 978-3-8174-7305-2

Komplott unter Palmen
ISBN 978-3-8174-7571-1

Schüsse im Nebel
ISBN 978-3-8174-7763-0

The Mystery of the Mummy
ISBN 978-3-8174-7304-5

Tod eines Dandys
ISBN 978-3-8174-7660-2

Toxic Testament
ISBN 978-3-8174-7879-8

Sammelband 3 in 1 (B1/B2)

Inspector Hudson Investigates
ISBN 978-3-8174-7625-1

London Crime Time
ISBN 978-3-8174-7787-6

B2

Bloody Diamonds
ISBN 978-3-8174-9494-1

Das geheimnisvolle Gemälde
ISBN 978-3-8174-7306-9

Der Seelenjäger
ISBN 978-3-8174-7581-0

Der unheimliche Ritter
ISBN 978-3-8174-7661-9

Die Rache des Lords
ISBN 978-3-8174-7663-3

Die Spur des Höllenhundes
ISBN 978-3-8174-7307-6

Lady Mayfair's Revenge
ISBN 978-3-8174-7815-6

Nobody Dies Twice
ISBN 978-3-8174-9495-8

Schatten der Vergangenheit
ISBN 978-3-8174-7570-4

The Riddle of the Black Shoe
ISBN 978-3-8174-7638-1

Business English

Der 25-Millionen-Coup
ISBN 978-3-8174-7659-6

Teuflische Intrigen
ISBN 978-3-8174-7608-4

C1/C2

A Scottish Murder Mystery
ISBN 978-3-8174-8379-2

Compact Lernkrimi
Kurzkrimis

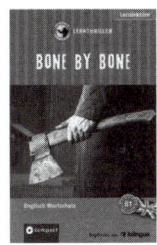

Compact Lernkrimi
Lernthriller

Compact Lernkrimi Kurzkrimis	Compact Lernkrimi Lernthriller	
Death at Land's End ISBN 978-3-8174-9658-7 **The Murderer Next Door** ISBN 978-3-8174-9438-5		**A1**
Blood and Breakfast ISBN 978-3-8174-7760-9 **Deadly Business** ISBN 978-3-8174-9215-2 **It Was Murder, My Lord** ISBN 978-3-8174-7734-0 **Last Exit Waterloo Bridge** ISBN 978-3-8174-7733-3 **Murder at Teatime** ISBN 978-3-8174-7839-2 **Sammelband 10 in 1 (A2/B1)** **Murderous Collection** ISBN 978-3-8174-8967-1		**A2**
Bullets over Bristol ISBN 978-3-8174-8544-4 **Death Comes Knocking** ISBN 978-3-8174-7945-0 **American Business English** **Murderous Network** ISBN 978-3-8174-9312-8	**Bone by Bone** ISBN 978-3-8174-9497-2 **Massacre United** ISBN 978-3-8174-9319-7 **American English** **Faceless Killer** ISBN 978-3-8174-8856-8	**B1**
	In Terror ISBN 978-3-8174-8857-5	**B2**
		C1/C2

Compact Lernkrimi
Rätselblock

Compact Lernkrimi
Hörbuch

	Compact Lernkrimi Rätselblock	Compact Lernkrimi Hörbuch
A1	**Murderous Games** ISBN 978-3-8174-9500-9	
A2	**The Art of Crime** ISBN 978-3-8174-9155-1	**A Shot in the Night** ISBN 978-3-8174-8202-3 **Death Wish** ISBN 978-3-8174-8204-7 **Strangled** ISBN 978-3-8174-9665-5 **The Butterworth Mystery** ISBN 978-3-8174-8203-0
B1	**A Deadly Puzzle** ISBN 978-3-8174-8832-2	**Bloody Revenge** ISBN 978-3-8174-8860-5 **Danger at King's Cross** ISBN 978-3-8174-7673-2 **The Thames Murderer** ISBN 978-3-8174-7674-9
B2		**Bloody Legacy** ISBN 978-3-8174-7676-3 **Die Intrigantin** ISBN 978-3-8174-7675-6 **Business English** **Crime & Company** ISBN 978-3-8174-8976-3 **Murder at the Office** ISBN 978-3-8174-7747-0
C1/C2		

Compact Lernkrimi
Audio-Learning

Compact Lernkrimi
Sprachkurs

	Englisch für Anfänger (A1/A2) ISBN 978-3-8174-7784-5	**A1**
		A2
Totenstille im Hyde Park ISBN 978-3-8174-7797-5		**B1**
		B2
		C1/C2

Compact Lernkrimi
Spannend Sprachen lernen

Compact Lernkrimi Classic

> Spannende Krimistory mit über 70 Übungen

> Vokabel- und Infokästen direkt auf der Seite

ab 7,99 € (D)

Compact Lernkrimi Kurzkrimis

> Drei bzw. vier Kurzkrimis pro Band

> Ideal für den Einsatz an Schulen und VHS-Kursen

7,99 € (D)

Compact Lernkrimi Lernthriller

> Hochspannende Thriller mit Gänsehaut-Garantie

> 70 Übungen in ansteigendem Schwierigkeitsgrad

> Vokabel- und Infokästen

7,99 € (D)

Compact Lernkrimi Sammelband

> Drei Lernkrimis in einem Band mit über 300 Übungen

> Für mittleres bis fortgeschrittenes Sprachniveau

12,99 € (D)

Compact Lernkrimi Hörbuch

> Krimistory auf CD mit MP3-fähigen Tracks

> Begleitbuch zum Mitlesen inklusive Übungen und Vokabelangaben

9,99 € (D)

Compact Lernkrimi Audio-Learning

> Spannende Story im Buch

> Übungen zu Hörverständnis und Aussprache auf CD

9,99 € (D)

Compact Lernkrimi Sprachkurs

> Sprachen lernen für Anfänger

> Krimigeschichte in 10 Lektionen

> Vokabelkarten zum kostenlosen Download

14,99 € (D)

Compact Lernkrimi Rätselblock

> 10 Mini-Krimis mit 90 Rätselübungen

> Lösungen und Vokabelangaben auf der Rückseite

> Zahlreiche Illustrationen

5,99 € (D)

>> Jeder Band inklusive Abschlusstest und Glossar

Englisch | Spanisch | Italienisch | Französisch | DaF | Schwedisch

www.lernkrimi.de
www.compactverlag.de